500

quick & easy dishes

500

quick & easy dishes

the ideal cookbook for new cooks, students, and people on the go!

Deborah Gray

SELLERS
PUBLISHING

A Quintet Book

Published by Sellers Publishing, Inc.
161 John Roberts Road, South Portland, Maine 04106
Visit our website: www.sellerspublishing.com
E-mail: rsp@rsvp.com

ISBN: 978-1-4162-4583-4
Library of Congress Control Number: 2016930061
QTT.FHSM

This book was conceived, designed and produced by
Quintet Publishing Limited
Ovest House
58 West Street
Brighton
BN1 2RA

Food Stylist: Valentina Harris
Photographer: Ian Garlick
Designer: Tania Gomes
Art Director: Michael Charles
Editorial Assistant: Ella Lines
Project Editors: Alice Sambrook, Leah Feltham
Editorial Director: Emma Bastow
Publisher: Mark Searle

10 9 8 7 6 5 4 3 2 1

Printed in China by 1010 Printing International Ltd.

contents

introduction

This book has been written with new cooks and busy people in mind. The recipes have been simplified to ensure success and reduce the ingredients you need to buy—but not at the cost of taste. Follow the instructions and you'll be surprised at how easy it is to produce delicious food, even if you're not an experienced cook. The book presumes you won't have the time or space for big shopping trips and uses a limited palette of ingredients. Most recipes only use only one burner on the stove at a time, because you may share a kitchen with others, and everyone always seems to cook at once! Cooking is an art, not a science, and most recipes are adaptable. Use what you have on hand or what you most enjoy eating, and substitute your favored ingredients for those less appealing to you. Most importantly, have fun in the kitchen.

cooking economically

Shopping wisely and using everything we buy, including leftovers, avoids wasting money and makes sound environmental sense.

It's a good idea to plan your meals and shop with the menu for a few days in mind. Many of the recipes in this book draw from a range of ingredients, so if you buy a jar of roasted red bell peppers, for instance, you'll find several ways to use them up without eating the same meal over and over. To minimize waste, be aware of what's to be used up and work your menu plan around that before shopping for more perishables. You'll soon get the hang of thinking up something to make with the multiple vegetable bits in the refrigerator—perhaps a soup, or buy a few shrimp and make a stir-fry.

Avoid the trap of false bargains that stores offer to entice us to buy more. Bulk buying is only a good deal if you use it all. Check the best-by dates to ensure you'll have time to use it. Also, try shopping late in the day to pick up bargains. But be sensible—it's great to buy one piece of fish for next to nothing, but buying four that end up stinking in the refrigerator or hiding in the freezer is a false economy. Be realistic about your eating capacity.

Buy food in markets and local and ethnic stores to find seasonal produce at good prices, and avoid the supermarket tyranny of the perfectly formed carrot and plastic packaging. Smaller suppliers are often happy to sell you smaller quantities, and often know their produce and how to cook it, so can offer cooking tips. But if you do shop at supermarkets, buy store brands rather than premium products, especially on items such as canned tomatoes and beans. And never shop when you are hungry.

healthy eating

Busy lifestyles aren't conducive to healthy eating — it's all too easy to rely on fast food and restaurant meals with friends, or to eat quick snacks and prepared meals high in salt, sugar, and saturated fats. The recipes in this book will provide you with some much healthier options, but there are some unhealthy treats too, like the chocolate brownies, which are high in sugar and fat. Ensure you don't make them every day, and that you eat your fair share of healthy dishes.

The advice around healthy eating changes, but the following outlines some basics.

the golden rules
Eat and drink the correct amount of food you need to sustain your lifestyle. Eating too much will cause you to put on weight; conversely, if you eat and drink too little, you'll lose weight. The average man needs around 2,500 calories a day. The average woman needs 2,000 calories. Most people eat more calories than they need. Remember, very few people are average.

Eat a wide range of foods to give you a balanced diet so your body receives all the nutrients it needs. Eating a range of fruits and vegetables of different colors is a good practice.

Proteins contain the essential amino acids needed to keep healthy. They are referred to as the building blocks of life and are found in every cell in the body. Include proteins in your diet by eating meat, fish, poultry, dairy products, and soy-based products. Beans, lentils, nuts, and cereals contain incomplete proteins, so a variety should be eaten if they are your only source.

Starchy foods (potatoes, cereals, pasta, rice, and bread) should make up one-third of your diet.

Choose whole-grain varieties and cook potatoes with skins on if possible; they contain more fiber and fill you up for longer. Include at least one starchy food with main meals. It's a myth that starchy foods are fattening — gram for gram they contain fewer than half the calories of fat.

Sugar is considered the main culprit behind the wave of obesity in our society. Sugary foods also cause tooth decay. Monitor your consumption of sugary and carbonated drinks, cakes, cookies, pastries, and sweets, and cut down, if necessary. You don't need to be so concerned about the sugars found naturally in foods such as fruit and milk. Food labels can help; use them to check how much sugar foods contain. More than 3/4 oz. (22.5 g) of sugar per 3 1/2 oz. (100 g) means the food is high in sugar. Alcoholic drinks are high in sugar, as are some fruit-based drinks such as smoothies.

Eat plenty of fruit and vegetables, at least five portions of different types a day. A glass of 100 percent unsweetened fruit juice counts as one portion (but only one glass counts per day). Beware of fruit juice drinks made from a mixture of fruit juices with added sugars.

Cut down on bad fats. There are two main types of fat: saturated and unsaturated. Too much of the former can increase the amount of cholesterol in the blood, which increases your risk of developing heart disease. Saturated fat is found in hard cheese, cakes, cookies, pies, the fat on red meat, processed foods, cream, and butter. Choose lean meat and cook with oil rather than butter. Eat foods that contain unsaturated fats, such as vegetable oils, oily fish, and avocados.

Nothing needs to be off limits. However, foods such as hamburgers, pizza, or pancakes shouldn't be eaten every day. You want to avoid eating these foods more than a couple of times a week at the very most. Consider things like chips or ice cream as an occasional treat, otherwise, there is a real risk of encountering weight problems.

cooking tips

- Measurements given in the recipes are for guidance only. Adjust seasonings and spices to your taste, add pasta to suit your appetite, or a couple of extra mushrooms, rather than leave them to go to waste. Likewise, substitute ingredients you like for those you don't, and vegetables you have for those specified, providing the texture and density are similar.

- Ovens vary in temperature, so use the recommended temperature as a guide and reduce the heat a little if you find your oven runs too hot. Use your eyes and nose to decide when something is cooked and never be afraid to test that meat is cooked by removing it from the pan and dissecting, or sticking a knife in a broccoli stem to check it is tender.

- Follow the instructions. If the recipe says "bring to a boil over a high heat, then simmer," do that or you'll have dried up, undercooked, or burned food.

- Recipes in this book use sunflower oil, but vegetable or canola oil are good substitutes. Olive oil is required where its flavor adds to the dish, but use the above alternatives if not available. Note: Oils kept in the refrigerator may go cloudy as they solidify slightly.

- The color of a fresh chile is no indication of it's fieriness; it is the thin, small chiles that pack the punch. Removing seeds and membranes will reduce the impact of a fresh chile.

- To skin tomatoes, make a score in the base of the tomato, cover with boiling water for 20 seconds, transfer to a bowl of cold water, then peel once cool enough to handle.

- 1 teaspoon dried herbs = 1 tablespoon chopped fresh herbs. Leftover fresh herbs can be chopped, put in ice cube trays and covered with a little water. Once frozen, store in a labelled zip-lock bag.

- Make salad dressings in a small screw-top jar.

- Use strong cheese in cooking. While Parmesan may seem expensive, you use a little of it; similarly use sharp Cheddar cheese. You need to use a good deal more mild cheese to add flavor and you are getting a lot of added fat into the bargain. You can store commercially grated Parmesan in the freezer and use it from frozen.

food safety hints and tips

- Keep your kitchen and your hands clean.
- Store cooked and uncooked food separately to prevent cross-contamination and wash your hands and cutting boards between handling cooked and uncooked foods. Meat and fish should be stored on the bottom shelf in the refrigerator to avoid them dripping into other foods.
- Always cool food before refrigerating.
- Freeze food as soon as possible after cooling, in sealed plastic containers or zip-lock bags, labeled and dated. Leave a gap in the box or bag for the liquid to expand as it freezes.
- Always defrost meat, seafood, and poultry before cooking to avoid the risk of food poisoning. However, shrimp are the exception to this rule.
- Store leftover canned food in airtight boxes or bags, not the cans, and eat within a few days.
- Reheated food should be very hot to kill any bacteria. Never reheat food more than once. Note: cooked rice is potentially hazardous if not consumed within 24 hours.
- Cover food or wrap in plastic wrap once opened to prevent drying out and contamination.
- Respect best-by dates and don't eat food that shows signs of mold or deterioration. Use your nose too — if it doesn't smell good, trash it.
- You are less likely to cut yourself with a sharp, effective knife.

cupboard essentials

- salt
- black pepper
- sunflower or vegetable oil
- balsamic vinegar
- cider vinegar
- soy sauce (preferably reduced-salt)
- ketchup
- French and whole-grain mustard
- mayonnaise
- tube or jar of garlic and/or ginger purée
- long-grain rice
- risotto (Arborio) rice
- dried pasta
- couscous
- bouillon cubes or powder
- canned tomatoes

- canned beans (e.g. cannellini, black, kidney, garbanzo)
- canned tuna and salmon
- canned or frozen corn
- frozen garden peas
- red lentils
- all-purpose flour
- baking soda
- baking powder
- cornstarch
- dried herbs (mixed herbs, oregano, basil)
- spices (ground cinnamon, turmeric, chili powder, paprika, red chili flakes, medium curry powder, Thai curry paste)
- honey
- sugar (superfine, brown sugar and confectioners' sugar for baking)
- jars of antipasto, roasted red bell peppers, olives
- teas and coffee

perishable supplies
- butter
- eggs
- onions
- garlic
- vegetables and fruit
- meat, fish, and chicken

basic equipment
- 2 or 3 sharp knives, including a serrated knife
- wooden spoons
- large spatula or fish slice
- potato masher
- garlic crusher
- pepper mill
- can opener
- vegetable peeler
- grater
- cutting board
- large mixing bowl
- strainer
- colander
- set of 2 or 3 saucepans
- non-stick skillet
- baking sheet
- medium roasting pan
- oven-proof and microwave-proof baking dishes
- stove top-proof casserole or similar
- measuring cups
- selection of airtight storage containers
- oven mitts
- kitchen towels
- assorted baking pans (as required)

using the microwave

Microwave cooking is great when you don't have a lot of time on your hands. So many people just use their microwave for heating up prepared food, but it's a versatile tool and many of the dishes in this book take advantage of the technology.

Microwave ovens transmit microwaves, which belong in the same category as radio signals, but at an ultra-high frequency. These waves bounce off the metal walls of the oven, penetrating the food and causing the liquid molecules to vibrate and heat up. Food will not heat in a metal container. Glass (not lead crystal), china, and some plastics are microwave safe.

Different manufacturers offer ovens that function at different wattages. These recipes are tested on a 1,000-watt machine; if yours is more or less, adjust timings accordingly.

The time taken to cook food in a microwave increases proportionately to any increase in quantity. As a rough guide, for double the quantity, add on half as much time again. So if one potato takes 5 minutes to cook, two will take 7 to 8 minutes.

Foods that have a fixed skin, like a potato, must be pierced before cooking to prevent steam building up inside and causing an explosion. An egg yolk is another example; it must be pierced a couple of times with a toothpick before microwave poaching.

Liquid foods must be stirred while cooking as food on the outside of the dish cooks quicker than that in the center of the dish.

Likewise, solid foods need turning. Be careful when stirring because some heated liquids can bubble without much warning. Similarly, many foods need to be covered to prevent splattering; a plate is good for this or use plastic wrap.

Food continues to cook for a few minutes after the oven has stopped and this is calculated into the cooking time.

a few basic recipes

Invest a little time into making a basic tomato and a béchamel sauce for the freezer, so a great pasta, meat or fish dish, or a yummy mac and cheese, is always available at the drop of a hat without resorting to cans or packets. And it's such a shame to throw out chicken bones, so use them to make a bouillon for a soup on another day. Once prepared, allow these dishes to cool, then package in individual portions in zip-lock bags, label, date, and freeze.

basic tomato sauce

A classic recipe, used as a base for many stews, pasta sauces, and soups.

For 4 Makes 2 cups	Bulk Makes 1 quart	Ingredients
2 tbsp.	1/4 cup	olive oil
1 medium	2 large	onion, chopped
1 small	2 large	carrot, grated
2 or 2 tsp.	8 or 2 1/2 tbsp.	medium garlic cloves, finely chopped
14 oz.	2 x 14 oz.	canned chopped tomatoes, drained
2 tbsp.	1/2 cup	tomato purée
1/4 cup	1 cup	red wine or juice from the tomatoes
1 tsp.	1 1/2 tbsp.	dried basil or oregano
		sea salt and black pepper

Heat the oil in a saucepan and add the onion and carrot. Cook gently over a low heat for 5 to 7 minutes until the onion is soft. Add the garlic and cook for 1 minute, then stir in the remaining ingredients. Season to taste. Cook for 10 minutes, or until the sauce has thickened. Leave the sauce chunky or purée with a hand-held blender.

basic béchamel sauce

The classic white sauce, this can be used as the basis of a creamy vegetable sauce. It's also good in a chicken or vegetable pie filling with ingredients such as spinach, mushrooms, ham, or seafood. For a cheese-style sauce, stir in 1 1/4 cups grated sharp Cheddar cheese after the sauce has thickened.

For 4 Makes 1 1/2 cups	Bulk Makes 1 1/2 quarts	Ingredients
2 tbsp.	1/2 cup (1 stick)	butter or margarine
3 tbsp.	3/4 cup	all-purpose flour
1 1/2 cups	1 1/2 quarts	milk
pinch	1/2 tsp.	ground nutmeg
		sea salt and white pepper

Melt the butter or margarine in a saucepan, stir in the flour and cook over a low heat for 2 minutes, stirring constantly. Slowly add the milk, then increase the heat slightly and bring to a boil, stirring until the sauce thickens. Add the nutmeg and season. For a dairy-free version, use soy margarine or 2 tablespoons sunflower or olive oil, and soy milk in place of cow's milk. For a reduced-fat version, use 2 tablespoons sunflower or olive oil and low-fat milk.

chicken bouillon

Make chicken bouillon from a chicken carcass and fresh vegetables, vegetables scraps, and peelings. Avoid using root ends, dirty scrapings, and starchy vegetables such as potatoes. Ensure a good mix of vegetables to avoid having a dominant flavor. This freezes well.

1 chicken carcass including the skin
1 large onion, roughly chopped
1 carrot, scrubbed and roughly chopped
1 stalk of celery, roughly chopped
vegetable peelings (see note, above)
1 garlic clove, chopped
2 bay leaves
1 bunch of fresh parsley
1/2 tsp. salt
1/2 tsp. whole peppercorns
water

Put the ingredients in a large pan and cover with water. Bring to a boil over a high heat, then simmer, uncovered, for at least 1 hour, preferably 2 or 3. Cool, skim off any visible fat, and strain. Use within 5 days or freeze. Makes approximately 1 quart.

For a vegetarian bouillon, omit the chicken bones and double the quantity of vegetables.

To save on freezer space, reduce the bouillon by half by boiling vigorously. Cool and pour into ice-cube trays. When frozen put the cubes into zip-lock bags. Then, when needed, simply pop a cube in a mug and add boiling water to dissolve the cube. Alternatively, freeze in small plastic boxes.

breakfasts & brunches

The brain cannot function efficiently without fuel, so it isn't sensible to skip breakfast, especially when you're starting a busy day. Of course, a bowl of cereal or a slice of toast will often be the quick and easy option, but this chapter includes some alternative ideas for quick, healthy breakfasts that will give you a boost in the morning. On the weekend, with a little more time to spare, you may want to indulge in one of the more substantial breakfast or brunch ideas here.

blueberry & oat pancakes

see variations page 30

These pancakes are simple to prepare and, as they are made with yogurt, orange juice, and oats, they are more nutritious and filling than most pancakes. Eat them on their own, with extra yogurt, or with added sweetness in the form of honey or maple syrup.

1 egg
1/2 cup yogurt
1/2 cup orange juice
1/2 tsp. vanilla extract (optional)
1/2 cup whole wheat flour
2 tbsp. superfine sugar

1 tsp. baking powder
1/4 tsp. baking soda
1/4 cup rolled oats
pinch of salt
1/2 cup blueberries
1/2–1 tbsp. sunflower oil

Break the egg into a bowl and, using a whisk or fork, beat in the yogurt, orange juice, and vanilla extract, if using. Beat in the flour, sugar, baking powder, baking soda, rolled oats, and salt until the mixture is smooth. Carefully stir in the blueberries.

Heat a medium-size skillet over a medium-high heat for a minute, and add just enough oil to lightly cover the base of the pan. Pour about 1/4 cup of the batter into the pan, then repeat, leaving enough space between each pancake to give them room to spread out slightly. Cook the pancakes for 2 to 3 minutes, or until small bubbles appear on the surface and the bases are golden. Then use a spatula to carefully flip them over. When the pancakes are golden on both sides, transfer to a plate. Repeat with the remaining batter. Alternatively, keep any remaining batter, covered with plastic wrap, in the refrigerator for 24 hours and stir well before using.

Makes about 10

chorizo–beans on toast

see variations page 31

This classy brunch-style beans on toast is one of those breakfast dishes that is lovely at any time of the day. The recipe makes a delicious home-cooked beans dish, but you could substitute a can of baked beans for a very quick alternative.

1 tbsp. olive oil, plus extra for drizzling
1 chorizo, thickly sliced
1 small onion, thinly sliced
1 garlic clove
14-oz. can cannellini (white kidney) or other
    beans, rinsed and drained
1 cup canned tomatoes

6 tbsp. chicken bouillon (made with
    1/4 bouillon cube)
1/4 tsp. mixed herbs
salt and pepper
4 thick slices of sourdough or
    whole wheat bread

Preheat the broiler on a high setting. Heat the oil in a pan over a medium-high heat. Add the chorizo and cook, stirring occasionally, for about 2 minutes, until lightly browned. Reduce the heat to medium, add the onion and cook, stirring occasionally, for about 5 minutes until soft and translucent. Meanwhile, cut the garlic clove in half lengthwise and finely chop one half, reserving the other half. Add the chopped garlic to the onion and cook for 1 minute. Add the beans, tomatoes, bouillon, and mixed herbs, season to taste and simmer for about 5 minutes, or until the liquid is reduced by half.

Meanwhile, lightly toast the bread on one side. Rub the uncooked side of the bread with the cut-side of the reserved garlic. Drizzle the bread slices with a little olive oil and broil, turning once, until golden. Top with bean mixture and serve hot.

Serves 2

scrambled egg pita

see variations page 32

This is a delicious way to eat your morning egg. The basic instructions given below for scrambled egg can easily be bulked up for more people and can be served on toast or alongside bacon and mushrooms.

1 egg
1 tbsp. milk
salt and pepper
1 tsp. butter

1 small tomato, chopped
chili sauce (optional)
1 pita bread

Beat the egg and milk with some salt and pepper in a bowl. Melt the butter in a skillet set over a medium-high heat, then pour in the egg and cook over a moderate heat for 20 seconds. Stir with a wooden spoon, taking care to move the cooked egg from the base of the pan as it cooks. Remove the pan from the heat just before the egg is completely set — it will continue to cook after it is removed from the heat. Stir in the chopped tomato and a dash of chili sauce, if using.

While cooking the egg, warm the pita bread. Cut it in half and gently separate the top and bottom layers of bread to form a pocket. Stuff with the scrambled egg.

Serves 1

french toast roll-ups

see variations page 33

These breakfast toasts are a special treat, yet are simple to make. You can prepare them the evening before you intend to eat them and leave them covered in the refrigerator, then all you have to do in the morning is cook them. The key to this recipe is to use soft white bread that rolls up easily and contains the filling without cracking.

1 large egg
2 tbsp. milk
3 tbsp. superfine sugar
1/2 tsp. ground cinnamon

8 slices of soft sandwich bread
8 tsp. strawberry conserve
8 strawberries or 2 bananas, thinly sliced
1 tbsp. butter

In a shallow dish, mix together the egg and the milk with a fork, and set aside. In a separate dish combine the sugar and cinnamon, and set aside.

Cut the crusts off the bread, then flatten out each piece with a rolling pin to remove any air pockets. Spread a little strip of conserve at one end of each piece of bread and top each with the strawberry or banana slices. Roll each one up like a jelly roll. Dip the roll-ups in the egg and milk mixture, turning carefully to ensure they are evenly coated.

Heat a skillet over a medium heat for 1 minute. Add the butter and, once melted, add the roll-ups with the seam side facing down to seal. Cook until golden brown, then turn and continue to cook until golden all over. Remove the rolls from the pan one at a time and roll in the sugar-cinnamon mixture to coat. Serve immediately.

Makes 8

overnight oatmeal with banana

see variations page 34

Breakfast couldn't be simpler. Just assemble the ingredients the night before and breakfast is ready in the morning. This raw oats recipe is served cold, which is super healthy because most of the nutrients are preserved. Including the fresh berries and nuts adds to the goodness, but they could be replaced by a little crunchy granola for texture. For a dairy-free version, use soy yogurt and soy or almond milk. Check out page 34 for a hot version.

1/4 cup rolled oats
1/3 cup Greek yogurt
1/3 cup milk
1/2 banana, mashed

to serve
1 tbsp. Greek yogurt
maple syrup
few almonds and fresh berries (optional)

In a 1 1/2-cup jar or a small bowl, mix together the oats, yogurt, milk, and mashed banana. Cover and refrigerate overnight.

In the morning, top with the additional yogurt and drizzle with maple syrup. Sprinkle with the almonds and fresh berries, if desired.

Serves 1

toasted bagel with
cream cheese & grapes

see variations page 35

This pretty variation on a bagel with cream cheese comes with the refreshing taste
of juicy grapes. If you haven't got any grapes on hand, try it with slices of peach or a
sweet, crunchy apple. It is so very simple to put together, but if you prepare this dish for
a friend, it will still look as if you have made an effort!

1 plain, raisin, blueberry, or mixed-seed bagel
3 tbsp. cream cheese (preferably low-fat)
pinch of ground cinnamon

10 black seedless grapes, halved
10 green seedless grapes, halved

Cut the bagel in half, then toast it on both sides, either in a wide-mouthed toaster or
under the broiler. Spread each half liberally with cream cheese. Top with a light dusting of
cinnamon and then with the halved grapes. Serve in 2 halves while the bagel is still warm.

Serves 1

tomato & avocado omelet

see variations page 36

This is one of those standard recipes that is useful to have in your repertoire for a last-minute meal, day or night. The variations on the fillings are limitless. Using this recipe, you can easily turn a few scraps of cheese, meat or vegetables into a satisfying, economical and nutritious meal. For instance, try this one with a little crumbled blue cheese, goat cheese or feta cheese, or with a few torn basil or arugula leaves.

2 eggs
1 tbsp. water
salt and black pepper

1 tbsp. butter
1 medium tomato, chopped
1/2 avocado, peeled, pitted and sliced

Break the eggs into a small bowl and beat with a fork until smooth. Stir in the water and season generously with salt and pepper.

Melt the butter in a medium skillet set over a medium-high heat, tilting to coat the bottom of the pan with melted butter. Pour in the beaten eggs and, using a spatula or the back of a fork, gently draw the mixture at the edge of the pan to the center as it sets and allow the liquid egg to flow into the spaces created. When almost set, add the chopped tomato and avocado to one half of the omelet and cook for 1 minute to heat through. Fold the omelet in half to cover the filling and serve immediately.

Serves 1

greek yogurt & berry breakfast

see variations page 37

This breakfast couldn't be easier to make or more refreshing to eat. It doubles as a quick dessert too, maybe using a berry-flavored yogurt. You could even layer it in a glass with muesli for an elegant fruit parfait. Greek yogurt is thicker and creamier than natural yogurt and contains up to twice as much protein and about half the carbohydrates. On the downside, it contains roughly one-third less calcium. It is also higher in fat, so take advantage of the reduced fat and fat-free varieties.

3/4 cup Greek yogurt
runny honey, to taste
6 strawberries, halved

1/4 cup blueberries
1 tbsp. mixed seeds (such as sunflower,
    pumpkin, sesame, and flax)

Put the yogurt in a cereal bowl or glass, and drizzle with honey, to taste. Top with the strawberries and blueberries and sprinkle over the seeds.

Serves 1

variations

blueberry & oat pancakes

see base recipe page 17

maple, banana & raisin pancakes
Omit the blueberries. Make the batter adding 1 small mashed banana and 2 tablespoons raisins with the orange juice. Serve with maple syrup.

maple & bacon pancakes
Omit the blueberries. Make the pancake batter, preferably with vanilla, and add 1 tablespoon maple syrup. Once the pancakes are cooked, cover with a clean kitchen towel and keep warm. Cook 4 slices of bacon in the same skillet until crisp. Serve the bacon with the pancakes, accompanied by maple syrup.

baby food pancakes
Omit the blueberries. Make the pancake batter adding 6 tablespoons applesauce, mango or other fruit purée to the mixture with the orange juice. (There are a good selection of fruit purée flavors in the baby food section of the supermarket.)

chocolate chip pancakes
Make the pancake batter using the vanilla and replacing the blueberries with 1/4 cup chocolate chips.

variations

chorizo–beans on toast

see base recipe page 18

bean & egg burrito
Make the bean mixture using black beans and add 1/2 to 1 teaspoon chili powder with the garlic, to taste. While cooking, beat an egg in a small bowl, pour into a lightly oiled hot skillet and cook on each side for 2 to 3 minutes until set and golden. Cut into strips. Substitute 4 flour tortillas for the toast. Divide the beans and egg between the tortillas. Turn in 2 of the sides, then roll up the tortilla to enclose the mixture.

curried beans with naan bread
Omit the chorizo and bread. Make the bean mixture, adding 1/2 to 1 teaspoon medium curry powder, to taste, with the garlic. Serve with warmed naan or other flat bread.

cheesy beans on toast
Make the bean mixture, adding 1 ball of mozzarella, chopped into small pieces, just before serving. This is delicious either with or without the chorizo.

penne with chorizo & beans
Make the bean mixture and omit the toast. Cook 2 1/4 cups penne pasta in plenty of boiling water for 10 to 12 minutes, or until just cooked. Divide between 2 bowls and top with the beans-and-chorizo mixture.

variations

scrambled egg pita

see base recipe page 21

scrambled egg & ham pita
Follow the instructions for the basic recipe, adding 1 slice of ham, chopped into bite-size pieces, with the tomato.

scrambled egg & cheese pita
Follow the instructions for the basic recipe. Before stuffing the pita bread, spread the inside generously with reduced-fat cream cheese or with herbed cream cheese.

scrambled egg & lox
Follow the instructions for the basic recipe, replacing the tomato and chili sauce with 2 tablespoons chopped smoked salmon pieces and, if available, 1 teaspoon chopped fresh chives.

scrambled egg & avocado pita
Follow the instructions for the basic recipe. Finely slice the flesh of half a peeled and pitted ripe avocado. Stuff the avocado slices into the pita pocket before adding the egg.

variations

french toast roll-ups

see base recipe page 22

nutella & banana french toast roll-ups
Prepare the basic recipe using Nutella, or similar chocolate spread, instead of strawberry conserve, and topping with a few thin slices of banana.

blueberry french toast roll-ups
Prepare the basic recipe using cream cheese instead of strawberry conserve, and topping with a row of fresh blueberries. You will need about 1/4 cup cream cheese and 1/3 cup blueberries.

orange french toast roll-ups
Prepare the basic recipe adding the grated zest of 1/2 orange to the egg and milk mixture. Use marmalade instead of conserve and omit the fresh fruit. Serve with segments of orange on the side.

french toast
Make up the egg and milk mixture as directed. Soak the slices of bread in the mixture (there will be sufficient for 3 or 4 slices, depending on the size of your loaf). Cook as per the main recipe until golden on both sides. Serve sprinkled with the sugar-cinnamon mixture and some fresh fruit.

variations

overnight oatmeal with banana

see base recipe page 24

hot overnight oatmeal with banana

Make the overnight oatmeal using 2/3 cup milk. In the morning, cook in the microwave on HIGH for 1 minute. Stir, and cook for another 30 to 45 seconds. Serve as directed in the basic recipe, omitting the yogurt.

overnight oatmeal with banana & peanut butter

Make the overnight oatmeal as directed in the basic recipe, adding 1 tablespoon peanut butter to the mixture. Serve as directed.

overnight oatmeal with dried fruit & nuts

Make the overnight oatmeal as directed in the basic recipe, omitting the banana and using instead 2 tablespoons each of dried cranberries, chopped walnuts, and chopped dates. Serve with fresh berries or sliced peach.

overnight steel-cut oatmeal with apple & raisins

Make the overnight oatmeal as directed in the basic recipe, using steel-cut oatmeal, which will be crunchier than rolled oats. Substitute 1/2 of an apple, grated, for the banana. Also stir in 1 tablespoon each of raisins and walnuts and a generous pinch of ground cinnamon. Serve with fresh berries.

toasted bagel with cream cheese & grapes

see base recipe page 25

english muffin with cream cheese & conserve
Replace the bagel with a toasted English muffin and omit the ground cinnamon and grapes. In a bowl, combine the cream cheese and 1 to 2 tablespoons strawberry conserve. Spread this over the muffin. Top with a few slices of banana or slices of strawberry. This works with blueberry, raspberry, or cherry conserve.

bagel with cream cheese, tomato & avocado
Omit the ground cinnamon and grapes. Top the bagel with a medium tomato, sliced, and the finely sliced flesh of 1/2 peeled and pitted ripe avocado. Add a few torn basil leaves, if available. Drizzle with a little balsamic vinegar, Tabasco or other hot sauce, if desired.

bagel with cream cheese & jalapeño
Omit the ground cinnamon and grapes. Toast a plain or seeded bagel as directed. Combine the cream cheese with 2 tablespoons finely chopped green bell pepper, 1 sliced jalapeño and salt and pepper to taste. Add 1 tablespoon chopped fresh cilantro, if available. Spread over the bagel and top with slices of tomato.

bagel with cheese & bacon
Omit the ground cinnamon and grapes. Toast a plain or seeded bagel as directed, and spread with cream cheese. While the bagel is toasting, broil or pan-fry 2 slices of bacon until crisp. Put the 2 halves of the bagel together with the bacon in the middle. Some people like to add up to 1 tablespoon conserve or Thai sweet chili sauce.

variations

tomato & avocado omelet

see base recipe page 27

mushroom omelet
Before cooking the omelet, heat 1 tablespoon butter in the skillet. Add 6 sliced chestnut or white mushrooms and fry over a medium-high heat, stirring occasionally, for 2 to 3 minutes, until tender. Tip out of the pan onto a warmed plate and keep warm. Adding a little chopped fresh parsley would be lovely. Use the mushroom filling instead of the tomato-avocado filling.

cheese & jalapeño omelet
Prepare the omelet as directed, adding 2 tablespoons grated Cheddar cheese and 1 chopped jalapeño with the tomato. Allow the cheese to just melt before folding the omelet in half. Serve with the uncooked avocado slices on top of the finished omelet.

spinach, tomato & feta omelet
Prepare the omelet as directed in the basic recipe, adding 3 tablespoons crumbled feta cheese and a small handful of baby spinach leaves with the tomato. Omit the avocado. Allow the cheese to just melt and the spinach to wilt before folding the omelet in half.

skinny, fluffy tomato omelet
Put 1 egg yolk in a bowl with the water and mix with a fork to combine. In a separate bowl, beat 2 egg whites until they form soft peaks (the consistency of lightly whipped cream). Gently fold the egg yolk mixture into the egg whites with a spatula. Proceed as directed in the basic recipe, using low-fat cooking spray instead of butter. Sprinkle salt and pepper over the cooking omelet. Add the tomato, but omit the avocado.

variations

greek yogurt & berry breakfast

see base recipe page 28

greek yogurt with muesli
Prepare the basic recipe, adding 1/4 cup muesli to the bowl or glass before adding the yogurt. The fruit is optional.

greek yogurt with peaches & pecans
Prepare the basic recipe, replacing the strawberries and blueberries with a sliced pitted peach and 2 tablespoons chopped pecans.

greek yogurt smoothie
In a food processor, or using a stick blender, blend together the yogurt, 1 tablespoon honey, 1/2 cup orange juice, the strawberries, and the blueberries. Omit the seeds. Other additions could include 1/2 teaspoon vanilla extract, 2 slices of avocado, 1 tablespoon protein powder, a small handful of spinach or 1 tablespoon unsweetened cocoa powder.

cottage cheese with honey & berries
Prepare the basic recipe, replacing the yogurt with cottage cheese or some cottage cheese with pineapple.

eating on the go

When you're out for the day, it's all too easy to end up in the fast food restaurant at lunchtime, or to nip into a store for a snack loaded with sugar and other ingredients that won't do you any favors. But with just a little forethought and preparation, you can leave home with a healthy lunch or snack that might be just the thing to help you resist the temptation of the burger bar. It's good for the wallet as well as your health.

no-bake energy bars

see variations page 52

These little energy bars are simplicity itself to make and way, way cheaper than buying similar bars from the store. Note that they are calorific, so don't have them too often!

3 tbsp. honey
2 tbsp. peanut butter
1/2 cup pecans

1/2 cup almonds
2 tbsp. mini chocolate chips

In a small bowl, melt the honey for 30 seconds in the microwave until just melted. Stir in the peanut butter. Let cool (to prevent melting the chocolate chips when you add them).

Line a small baking pan with parchment paper.

Mix the remaining ingredients into the honey and peanut butter mixture thoroughly. Press the mixture firmly into the prepared pan. Refrigerate for at least 1 hour to set, then slice into six pieces. Store in the refrigerator. Wrap the bars tightly in plastic wrap or tin foil to transport.

Serves 6

hummus, pepper & carrot wrap

see variations page 53

This healthy wrap makes a great midday filler and requires less time to make than it takes to queue up to pay in a sandwich store during a busy lunchtime.

3 tbsp. hummus
1 wrap
few drops of lemon juice
pinch of ground cumin (optional)

1 small carrot, grated
1-in. (2.5-cm.) strip of red bell pepper, sliced
small handful of salad leaves

Spread the hummus over the wrap. Sprinkle with a few drops of lemon juice and a pinch of cumin, if using. Scatter the carrot and pepper over the hummus with the salad leaves. Roll up the wrap tightly, then cut into 2 to 3 pieces.

Wrap in plastic wrap or tin foil to transport. If not taking immediately, keep refrigerated until it's time to leave.

Serves 1

big beef sandwich

see variations page 54

This is like the deli sandwich that makes you drool with desire. It has plenty of meat and a lot of flavor. Using lean roast beef keeps this sandwich relatively low in fat, yet high in protein. Other meats, such as ham, salami, and pastrami, are higher in fat and/or sodium. This sandwich is made with two slices of bread, but it is equally good when made with a baguette, panini, or any other substantial bread roll.

2 thick slices of whole wheat, rye,
   or sourdough bread
1 tsp. butter or low-fat spread
1 tbsp. whole-grain mustard, horseradish,
   or mango chutney

2 slices of lean roast beef
2 tbsp. shaved Parmesan cheese or
   Cheddar cheese
1–2 sweet dill pickles, sliced
2 iceberg lettuce leaves

Spread 1 slice of bread with the butter or low-fat spread, and set aside. Spread the other slice with the mustard (or use horseradish or mango chutney if preferred). Top with half the roast beef, the cheese, the dill pickle, and the lettuce, then finish with the remaining meat. Sandwich together with the second slice of bread.

Slice in half and wrap tightly in waxed paper, plastic wrap, or tin foil. Refrigerate until ready to set off in the morning.

Serves 1

frittata

see variations page 55

This is a fabulous portable snack made with eggs and leftover potatoes. No potatoes?
No problem! You can use whatever vegetables you have in the refrigerator. Peppers,
mushrooms, chopped tomatoes, and zucchini would all work well. The frittata can be
eaten hot, warm, or at room temperature. Allow it to cool completely after cooking,
then cut it and wrap it in waxed paper and slip it into a plastic bag for transporting.

1 tsp. olive oil
1 tsp. butter
1 medium cooked potato, sliced
3 eggs

1/4 cup grated Parmesan or 1/2 cup grated
    Cheddar or crumbled feta cheese
2 scallions, sliced
snipped fresh chives, to garnish (optional)

Coat the base and sides of a small ovenproof skillet with the olive oil and butter. Put the
potato slices into the skillet and cook over a medium heat until they are just golden brown,
turning once.

Meanwhile, in a bowl, beat the eggs and stir in the cheese and scallions. Pour the egg
mixture over the potatoes, shaking the pan to allow it to seep between the potato slices.
Cook over a low heat for 8 to 10 minutes. The frittata should be firm underneath and slightly
loose on top. Using a wide spatula, peel back one side to lift it off the base of the pan, then
gently flip the frittata and cook until the underside is set. If you don't want to risk turning it,
you can put the skillet under a preheated broiler for 2 to 3 minutes to set the top. Garnish
with snipped chives, if using, to serve.

Serves 2

rustic chicken pasta salad

see variations page 56

This is a great meal to take on a picnic or to have for a lunch on the go. It uses salad dressing rather than mayonnaise as it is safer to eat if left unrefrigerated for a while. The ingredients given are guidelines — you can mix and match to suit your tastes and the contents of your cupboard. Pasta doubles in quantity when cooked. If a small mugful of cooked pasta in the salad isn't enough for you, cook more.

1/2 cup pasta bows or penne
2 tbsp. Italian salad dressing
1/2 tbsp. pesto (optional)
2 tbsp. finely chopped red onions or
    2 scallions, finely chopped
2 tbsp. chopped sun-dried tomatoes

2 tbsp. canned corn
6 cherry tomatoes, halved
1/2 small zucchini, diced
8 oz. boneless, skinless chicken breasts, broiled,
    cut into 1/4-in.- (5-mm-) thick slices
shaved Parmesan cheese (optional)

Bring a pan of lightly salted water to a boil. Add the pasta and cook for 8 to 10 minutes until just cooked (al dente). Do not overcook. Drain and rinse in cold water, then let cool.

Mix together the cooled pasta, salad dressing, and pesto, if using. Gently mix in the remaining ingredients except the Parmesan cheese. Transfer to a plastic container and sprinkle over the cheese, if using — it may get tossed into the salad while transporting, but this doesn't matter.

Serves 2

not quite one-thousand-year-old eggs

see variations page 57

This is a tasty variation of the hard-boiled egg — the veteran of many a packed lunch or picnic. This recipe also gives you the timing for hard-boiled eggs; for runny, soft-boiled eggs, remove the eggs from the water after 3 minutes.

2 eggs
1/4 cup soy sauce or tamari
1/4 cup water or black tea

1 in. (2.5 cm.) fresh gingerroot, sliced
2 tbsp. granulated or superfine sugar

Put the eggs in a pan and cover with water. Bring to a boil over a medium-high heat, then reduce heat to low, cover and cook, just simmering, for 10 minutes. Drain, then run cold water over the eggs until cooled. To peel, crack the shell, then gently roll the egg on the work surface. Peel, then rinse under cold water to remove any stray bits of shell.

In a small pan, combine the soy sauce, water (or tea), ginger, and sugar, and bring to a simmer over a medium heat, stirring constantly, until the sugar is dissolved. Remove the pan from the heat and add the eggs. Using a spoon, roll them around gently in the soy mixture for about 15 minutes until the eggs have an even brown color, then leave to sit in the mixture for 1 hour, turning occasionally. Remove the eggs from the pan and let cool, then wrap them in plastic wrap to transport. These eggs can also be eaten warm, maybe with a noodle-and-vegetable stir-fry.

Serves 1

minted falafel pita pockets

see variations page 58

Store-bought falafel make great sandwiches. Stuff them into pita pockets with salad vegetables and you are in for a lunchtime treat. Ideally, use fresh mint to make the sauce, but dried mint is acceptable, especially if you are not eating immediately, as it gives the dried mint time to rehydrate. Remember to drain any excess liquid from the salad ingredients, to minimise the risk of soggy sandwich syndrome.

1 pita bread
4-6 falafel, depending on size
1 medium tomato, sliced
1 in. (2.5 cm.) cucumber, sliced
lettuce leaves, sliced

mint-yogurt sauce
2 tbsp. Greek yogurt
1/4 tsp. lemon juice
1/4 tsp. olive oil
1 tbsp. fresh mint or 1/2 tsp. dried mint
pinch of salt

In a small bowl combine all the ingredients for the mint-yogurt sauce. Set aside.

Cut the pita in half and gently separate the top and bottom layers of bread to form a pocket. Stuff with the falafel, tomato, cucumber and lettuce leaves. Drizzle over the sauce. The sauce can be put in a small, sealed container and taken separately, then drizzled over the sandwich just before you eat, if preferred.

Serves 1

mango & bean quinoa salad

see variations page 59

Quinoa is a grain native to South America that has a delicious nutty flavor and crunchy texture. In addition, it is rich in complete protein, making it an ideal food to eat on the go. Quinoa quadruples in size when cooked, so you will have some to spare for another meal, but it is hard cooking less than this quantity. This salad is suitable for vegans.

1 cup water
1/2 cup quinoa
1 cup canned kidney or mixed beans
3 scallions, sliced

2 stalks of celery, sliced
1/2 mango, peeled, pitted, and chopped
grated zest and juice of 1 lime
1 tbsp. olive oil

Salt the water and bring it to a boil in a medium saucepan. Rinse the quinoa, then add it to the pan. Stir and simmer for about 12 minutes, until tender and the germ ring inside the grain becomes visible. Drain, then cover with a clean kitchen towel and leave to sit for 5 minutes.

Put the cooked quinoa (or as much as you will eat) into a bowl. Drain the kidney beans, then add them to the bowl with the scallions, celery, and mango. Stir in the lime zest and juice and the olive oil. Pack the mixture into a portable container. It will keep for 24 hours in the refrigerator.

Serves 2

variations

no-bake energy bars

see base recipe page 39

sour cherry energy bars
Make the energy bars as directed using 6 tablespoons each of pecans, almonds, and sour cherries.

chocolate-drizzled energy bars
Make the energy bars as per the basic recipe. Break 1 ounce bittersweet chocolate into pieces and put it into a small bowl or mug. Melt in the microwave on low for about 1 1/2 minutes — the exact time will depend on your microwave. It is best to do this in bursts of 20 seconds, stirring between bursts, to avoid overheating. Drizzle the melted chocolate over the completed energy bars before chilling.

granola cereal bars
Replace the nuts with 1/2 cup granola and proceed as directed in the basic recipe.

seedy energy bars
Make the energy bars as directed, adding 1 tablespoon mixed seeds to the mixture.

hummus, pepper & carrot wrap

see base recipe page 40

hummus, egg & carrot wrap
Hard-boil an egg and allow it to cool (page 47). Peel and slice the egg, then lay the slices over the hummus. Proceed as directed.

guacamole wrap
Substitute guacamole for the hummus. Proceed as directed.

hummus, roasted pepper & olive wrap
Substitute half a well-drained roasted pepper from a jar for the red bell pepper. Add 4 sliced black olives. Proceed as directed. Other favorite antipasto cupboard ingredients such as artichokes or canned asparagus could replace the roasted peppers.

hummus & chicken tomato wrap
Lay thin slices of leftover chicken or a slice of deli chicken over the hummus. Replace the red bell pepper with 1 medium sliced tomato. Proceed as directed.

big beef sandwich

see base recipe page 43

big turkey sandwich
Replace the beef with turkey and use French mustard as the condiment. A slice of Swiss cheese works well instead of the Parmesan cheese.

big cheese-and-slaw sandwich
Replace the beef with slices of Cheddar, Gorgonzola, Edam or Emmental. Omit the Parmesan. Use 2 tablespoons coleslaw, draining off excess liquid, instead of pickles. (See page 146 for a recipe for quick coleslaw.) Omit the dill and mustard.

big fish sandwich
Replace the beef with a can of sardines in oil, thoroughly drained. Gently cut the sardines in half lengthwise with the blade of a knife to flatten slightly (you can eat the soft bones) before assembling the sandwich. Replace the pickles with 4 sliced sundried tomatoes. Omit the dill and mustard.

club sandwich
In a skillet over a medium-high heat, fry 2 slices of bacon until crisp. Remove from the pan and drain on paper towels, then let cool. Cut each slice in half. Make the turkey sandwich above using mayonnaise instead of butter. Omit the cheese and add 2 large tomato slices and the bacon. Omit the dill and mustard.

frittata

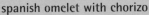

see base recipe page 44

spanish omelet with chorizo
Add 4 ounces sliced chorizo when frying the potatoes. The chorizo will produce quite a bit of fat, so dab with a paper towel to remove a little of the excess before adding the egg — don't remove it all because it is very tasty. Cook as directed.

roasted pepper frittata
Add 1 chopped roasted pepper from a jar to the skillet once the potatoes are cooked. Add 1/4 teaspoon paprika to the egg mixture. Proceed as directed.

sweet potato & spinach frittata
Use leftover sweet potatoes instead of regular potatoes. Once the potatoes are browned, add 3/4 cup frozen spinach and cook until the spinach has wilted and the liquid has evaporated. Proceed as directed.

mexican frittata
Once the potatoes are browned, add 1/4 teaspoon chili powder and cook for 1 minute. Add 1 chopped medium tomato, 1/2 sliced fresh jalapeño pepper and 4 tablespoons frozen or canned corn. Proceed as directed. Mozzarella is a good cheese to choose for this variation.

variations

rustic chicken pasta salad

see base recipe page 46

rustic tuna pasta salad
Replace the chicken with 1 cup canned tuna in water, drained and broken into chunks.

rustic mozzarella pasta salad
Replace the chicken with 1 ball of mozzarella cheese, torn into pieces.

tortellini pasta salad
Replace the pasta with 4 to 6 ounces packaged chilled tortellini. Choose a vegetarian tortellini if you are to carry this salad around unrefrigerated.

creamy pasta salad
Replace the Italian dressing with ranch, caesar or blue cheese dressing.

not quite one-thousand-year-old eggs

see base recipe page 47

hard-boiled eggs with celery salt

Follow the instructions for hard-boiled eggs, but do not peel – the shell is nature's packaging. Pour 1 teaspoon celery salt in a little paper or tin foil and twist to secure. To eat, peel the egg and dip it in the salt. Omit the last 4 ingredients.

hard-boiled eggs with olive oil & paprika

Follow the instructions above, omitting the celery salt. Combine in a small sealed plastic container 1/2 tablespoon olive oil, 1/4 teaspoon paprika and a generous pinch of salt. Use the oil mixture as a dip when eating the egg.

egg sandwich

Follow the instructions for hard-boiled eggs, above, omitting the other ingredients. Peel and roughly mash 2 hard-boiled eggs with a fork. Combine with 2 tablespoons finely chopped scallions or dill pickle. Mix with just enough mayonnaise to bind. Spread over a large slice of bread, top with shredded iceberg lettuce or watercress, and then top with another slice of bread.

thousand-year-old egg noodle salad

Make a salad from 1 handful each of spinach and beansprouts plus 2 handfuls of cooked rice noodles. Toss in 4 sliced water chestnuts from a can and 2 sliced not quite one-thousand-year-old eggs. For the dressing, combine 1 1/2 tablespoons olive oil, 1 tablespoon soy sauce, 1 teaspoon each of honey, vinegar, and water, and 1/4 teaspoon each of ginger purée and garlic purée.

variations

minted falafel pita pockets

see base recipe page 49

minted garbanzo pita pockets
Replace the falafel with 1/4 cup well-drained garbanzo beans.

minted feta pita pockets
Replace the falafel with 1/4 cup diced feta cheese, well drained. Many supermarkets
sell marinated feta with herbs, which is delicious.

falafel & arugula pita pockets
Replace the lettuce with arugula.

falafel take-out salad
Put all the salad ingredients and the falafel into a plastic container. (This also works well
with the garbanzo or feta variations.) Either dress with the mint–yogurt sauce or take this
in a separate sealed container. You could take the pita to eat on the side.

mango & bean quinoa salad

see base recipe page 50

mango & smoked turkey quinoa salad
Add 1 cup chopped smoked turkey to the salad.

peach & smoked ham quinoa salad
Add 1 cup chopped smoked ham to the salad and replace the mango with a peeled, pitted and chopped peach. If you are using peach from a can, select peaches in natural juice and drain well.

mixed vegetable quinoa salad
While the quinoa is cooking, cook 1 1/2 cups mixed frozen vegetables in boiling water. Drain and cool, then add to the quinoa instead of the beans, scallions, and celery.

curried mango & bean quinoa salad
Follow the basic recipe, but mix into the lime 3/4 teaspoon medium curry powder, 1/2 tablespoon mango chutney and a pinch of salt. (If you don't have mango chutney, use 1 teaspoon honey or maple syrup.) Replace the celery with 4 in. (10 cm.) cucumber, chopped.

10-minute meals

When time is short, ten minutes is sometimes all you can spare to fix something to eat. Here are a few ideas for such occasions so you don't resort to fast food. Instead, why not fix a good sandwich with the filling spread evenly all the way through (unlike many premade sandwiches), or try its heated Mexican cousin, a cheesy quesadilla, which can be made in a flash? Or you could cook a pasta or noodle dish in ten minutes with the right ingredients.

quesadilla with tomato, cheese & chili sauce

see variations page 81

This dish makes a great emergency snack — the tasty little sandwiches take no time to prepare and cook. Serve them alone or accompanied by guacamole or spicy dip. Use the remaining tortillas to make wraps or to eat with chili. Reseal the package using sticky tape or transfer to a zip-lock bag and keep for a couple of days. Alternatively, freeze for use another time.

2 soft flour tortillas
1/2 cup grated Cheddar cheese

2 medium tomatoes, chopped
2 tsp. Thai chili sauce or other chili sauce

Put 1 tortilla flat on your work surface. Sprinkle over the grated cheese and chopped tomato. Drizzle 1 teaspoon chili sauce over the cheese and tomatoes. Top with the other tortilla to enclose the cheese and tomato. Press down slightly.

Heat a large skillet (one that is large enough to hold the tortilla) over a medium-high heat. Using a wide spatula or working carefully by hand, transfer the tortilla to the hot pan and cook for about 2 minutes or until it turns crisp and golden. Turn and cook the second side. The cheese should now be melted and holding the quesadilla together. Transfer to a board or plate and cut in half, then cut each half into two or three triangles.

Serves 1–2

ham, garden pea & pesto linguine

see variations page 82

A packet of fresh pasta is just the thing to pick up on the way home when you're feeling very hungry. It cooks in minutes, giving you just enough time to assemble a few ingredients to toss into the bowl for a tasty meal. You will probably cook a quarter to a third of a 1-pound packet. Divide the remaining pasta into portions and put them in plastic bags, then seal and freeze them. When needed, cook the pasta from frozen — it takes only about a minute longer.

4 oz. fresh linguine
3 tbsp. frozen garden peas
1/4 cup cooked ham or Parma-style ham
6 cherry tomatoes

2 tsp. pesto (store-bought is fine)
salt and pepper
grated Parmesan or Cheddar cheese,
    to serve

Bring a pan of water to a boil. Add the linguine and peas, and cook for 3 to 4 minutes until the pasta is just tender (al dente).

Meanwhile, tear or chop the ham into small pieces. Chop the cherry tomatoes in half.

Drain the pasta and peas, stir in the pesto, then toss in the ham and cherry tomatoes, and season to taste with salt and pepper. Serve sprinkled with the grated cheese.

Serves 1

mozzarella & tomato salad

see variations page 83

This salad is often served as an appetizer in Italian restaurants under the name "insalata caprese" — it was originally served on the island of Capri as a tastebud-tingling light lunch. It looks particularly nice with multicolored tomatoes. You can serve it with some chunky bread or mix it into some leftover pasta if you need something more sturdy, and the recipe is easy to bulk up for guests.

6 oz. tomatoes (either 1 large or several
   small tomatoes)
4 oz. fresh mozzarella, cut into
   1/4-in.- (5-mm.-) thick slices

few fresh basil, parsley, or arugula leaves
1/4 tsp. dried oregano
1 tbsp. extra-virgin olive oil
salt and black pepper

Prepare the tomatoes as appropriate (slices for large or medium tomatoes; the small ones are best cut in half).

On a plate, arrange the tomatoes, mozzarella slices and basil, parsley, or arugula leaves, alternating and overlapping them. Sprinkle the salad with oregano and drizzle with oil. Season with salt and pepper.

Serves 1

chicken not-pot-noodle

see variations page 84

This really is the ultimate quick meal—it will take you just a few minutes to prepare the vegetables, then pour over boiling water and leave this meal to "cook" on its own. Make sure that you choose noodles that will soften in boiling water without the need for cooking. Providing you have access to boiling water, you can prepare the ingredients in a canning jar or conserve jar and take them with you for lunch—leave out the lemon juice and just pop a lemon wedge into the jar to squeeze over at the last moment instead.

1 nest of quick-cook thin egg noodles or
   vermicelli
1/4 cup shredded cooked chicken
1/4 tsp. chicken bouillon powder or
   1/4 crumbled bouillon cube
1 small carrot, coarsely grated
2 scallions, trimmed and finely sliced
1/4 cup frozen or canned corn or garden peas

10 baby spinach leaves, finely sliced
1/2 tsp. ginger purée (optional)
1/2 tsp. garlic purée (optional)
generous pinch of black pepper
1 tsp. soy sauce
squeeze of lemon juice

Put all the ingredients, except the lemon juice, in a covered heatproof bowl or jar. Pour over enough boiling water to just cover everything and press the ingredients down into the water with the back of a spoon.

Cover and leave for 8 minutes, stirring once. Stir in the lemon juice. Eat from the jar or transfer to a pasta bowl.

Serves 1

turkey & avocado sandwich

see variations page 85

A good sandwich has all the components of a good meal. This one has protein in the form of turkey and cream cheese, vitamins, and minerals in the raw vegetables, and fiber in the bread.

2 tbsp. low-fat cream cheese
2 thick slices of whole wheat or rye bread
1 slice of roasted turkey
1/4 avocado, thinly sliced

4 slices of tomato
2 iceberg lettuce leaves, shredded
1 tbsp. cranberry sauce (optional)

Spread the cream cheese on one side of both the slices of bread. Top one slice with turkey, avocado, tomato, and lettuce.

Spread cranberry sauce on top of the cream cheese on the other slice of bread, and sandwich the 2 halves together. Cut in half to serve.

Serves 1

spicy pepperoni french bread pizza

see variations page 86

This is one of those extremely versatile meals that can be made from whatever you have on hand. Individual or small French bread sticks are often reduced in price in the supermarket, so grab a couple when you have the chance and stick them in the freezer. If you haven't got any French bread rolls, panini makes a good substitute.

1 individual French bread roll
2 tbsp. tomato purée or tomato sauce
1/4 tsp. dried basil or oregano
pinch of red chili flakes

heaping 1/4 cup grated Cheddar cheese
1 small tomato, sliced
12 thin slices of pepperoni
black pepper

Preheat the broiler on a medium-high setting.

Cut the French bread in half and spread the tomato purée or sauce over the cut surfaces. Sprinkle with the dried basil or oregano and the chili flakes, then sprinkle with the grated cheese. Top with the slices of tomato and pepperoni. Season with black pepper.

Broil the pizzas for 2 to 4 minutes, or until the cheese begins to bubble and turn golden.

Makes 1 large or 2 small servings

lemon fish

see variations page 87

Fish is so quick and easy to cook and is wonderfully healthy, too. If you haven't cooked it before, this is a great recipe to start with. The recipe provides both broiling and microwaving instructions. If you use a thicker piece of fish, such as halibut, you will need to add a couple of minutes to the cooking time. The classic accompaniment to this dish is wilted spinach and a few boiled new potatoes.

1 tbsp. olive oil
2 white fish fillets such as cod, haddock,
    whiting, or sole
salt and pepper

juice of 1/2 lemon
1/4 tsp. grated lemon zest
1/4 tsp. paprika
chopped fresh parsley

Brush your broiler pan or microwave-safe dish with oil. Put your fish fillets on the pan and season. Drizzle with the remaining oil and the lemon juice and sprinkle over the grated zest.

To broil: Preheat the broiler on a high setting. Cook for about 5 minutes without turning, but baste with the lemon juice 3 times. The fish is cooked when it turns opaque and flakes easily.

To microwave: When arranging the fish in the dish, put the thickest side facing the outside of the dish and tuck under any very thin bits. Cover and cook on HIGH for 3 minutes. If the fish is not opaque throughout, cook for another 1 to 2 minutes, checking every 20 seconds.

Sprinkle paprika and parsley over the cooked fish to serve.

Serves 2

power-up roughie

see variations page 88

A roughie is a smoothie made without a blender. If you have a blender then, by all means, use it to turn this into a smoothie. These drinks offer a great way to recharge the batteries in the middle of the working day, or to soothe the system if you have been over-doing it! Any squashable fruit can be substituted for the banana (see the variations on page 88 for ideas).

1 medium ripe banana, peeled
1/4 cup plain low-fat yogurt

about 1 cup orange and mango juice
runny honey

Slice the banana and put it into a bowl, then mash it to a really smooth paste with a fork. Add the yogurt and use the fork to thoroughly mix the banana and yogurt together. Transfer the mixture to a large glass. Pour in enough orange and mango juice to fill the glass by about three quarters, then carefully stir the mixture with the fork until combined. Add honey to taste. Top off the glass with orange and mango juice as necessary.

If you have a blender, blend all the ingredients together and pour into a glass.

Serves 1

bean & tomato pantry soup

see variations page 89

This soup is almost as quick to make as packet soup, but it is much more wholesome and satisfying and doesn't have that synthetic flavor that you find with many commercial soups. You can enjoy this soup chunky, or if you have a stick blender, you can blend it until smooth.

1 tbsp. olive oil
1 medium onion, chopped
1 small garlic clove, crushed
14-oz. can puréed tomatoes
14-oz. can cannellini (white kidney)
   or other white beans

1/2 cup water
1 tbsp. soy sauce
1 tsp. Worcestershire sauce
2 tsp. mixed dried herbs, parsley, or oregano
salt and pepper
yogurt or grated cheese, to serve

Heat the olive oil in a medium-sized saucepan over a medium heat. Add the onion and garlic and cook for 4 minutes, stirring twice.

Put all the remaining ingredients, except the yogurt or grated cheese, into the saucepan. Blend with a stick blender, if you have one. Bring to a boil and simmer for 3 minutes. Serve in bowls topped with a spoonful of yogurt or some grated cheese, as preferred.

Serves 2–3

stir-fry shrimp with noodles

see variations page 90

The stir-fry is the best meal for busy people — it's made in minutes and is both filling and healthy. Tossing in some egg or rice noodles gives you a full and balanced meal from grocery bag to mouth in ten minutes. The recipe calls for a pak choi, which is just the right size for one. However, you could use half a packet of stir-fry vegetables instead. Generally, prepared vegetables are comparatively expensive, but for a stir-fry they provide a great variety of ready-sliced ingredients.

2 1/2 cups thin egg or rice noodles
1 tbsp. sunflower oil
1/2 mild red chile, sliced
1/2 in. (1 cm) fresh gingerroot, peeled,
    and thinly sliced
1 small garlic clove, finely chopped

1/4 red bell pepper, thinly sliced
2 scallions, thinly sliced
1 small pak choi, thinly sliced
1 cup small uncooked shrimp, shelled
    and deveined
1-2 tbsp. soy sauce

Bring a pan of water to a boil, then remove the pan from the heat and add the noodles. Leave them in the water to rehydrate or warm through, according to the packet directions.

Heat a wok over a high heat until very hot. Add the oil and swirl to coat. Add the chile, ginger and garlic, and stir-fry for 30 seconds. Add the pepper and scallions, and stir-fry for a further 30 seconds. Then add the pak choi and shrimp and stir-fry for 2 to 3 minutes, or until the shrimp are cooked. Toss in about 1 tablespoon water and enough soy sauce to coat the vegetables, and cook for 1 minute. Drain the noodles, transfer to a large bowl or plate and top with the stir-fry.

Serves 1

big mushroom sandwich

see variations page 91

Portabello mushrooms make a great vegetarian alternative to a regular burger. Select one roughly the same size as your bread roll (the really huge ones take longer to cook and will hang over the edge of the bread rather inelegantly). See the variations on page 91 for ideas for mushroom sandwiches made with smaller mushrooms.

1 portabello mushroom
1 1/2 tsp. olive oil
few drops of balsamic vinegar
pinch of red chili flakes
pinch of dried oregano or thyme

salt and pepper
1 garlic clove, cut in half lengthwise
1 ciabatta or crusty white roll, split
1 small tomato, sliced
lettuce or baby spinach leaves, cut into strips

Preheat the broiler on a high setting. Cut off the mushroom stem. Wipe the cap with damp paper towels. Put 1 teaspoon olive oil and the vinegar into the palm of your hand and smooth the mixture over the mushroom on all sides. Put the mushroom, stem-side up, on some tin foil or a small heatproof dish and sprinkle over the chili flakes, herbs, salt, and pepper. Place the mushroom under the broiler 3 to 4 inches (7.5 to 10 cm) from the heat and cook for 6 to 8 minutes, or until tender, turning half way through the cooking time.

Meanwhile, rub the cut side of the garlic on the cut surfaces of the bun. Drizzle with the remaining oil. Put the bun under the broiler with the mushroom and toast until golden. Put the cooked mushroom on the toasted bun and top with the tomato and lettuce or spinach.

Serves 1

chicken & black bean tacos

see variations page 92

This is one of those dishes that is always comforting. It bulks up easily, too, so it is a good one to make when someone stops by for a quick something to eat. The list of additions at the end of the ingredients is quite long — use any of them that you have on hand, in any combination.

sauce
3/4 cup puréed tomatoes
1 tsp. vinegar
1/2–1 tsp. chili powder
1/2 tsp. ground cumin
1 tsp. dried oregano
pinch of sugar

1 tbsp. sunflower oil
1 chicken breast, thinly sliced
salt and pepper
1/4 x 14-oz. can black beans, rinsed and drained
4 taco shells
1/4 cup grated Cheddar cheese
toppings: shredded lettuce, avocado wedges, sliced
    tomatoes, lime wedges, finely chopped onion, sliced
    cucumber, chopped fresh cilantro, to serve (all optional)
1/4 cup sour cream or Greek yogurt, to serve

Mix all the sauce ingredients in a small bowl and set aside. Heat a wok or skillet over a high heat until very hot. Add the oil and swirl to coat. Season the chicken with salt and pepper. Stir-fry for 3 to 4 minutes, or until cooked and white throughout. Pour in the sauce and beans and bring to a boil, then simmer for 3 minutes.

To serve, spoon the mixture into the taco shells and top with the cheese and any of the desired toppings, finishing with the sour cream or yogurt.

Makes 4

cheese & tomato soufflé in a mug

see variations page 93

This is a cunning little recipe for a sophisticated soufflé made in a large coffee mug and quickly cooked in the microwave (to cook in the oven, bake in an ovenproof dish for 15 to 20 minutes at 350°F/175°C). To make two mugs, multiply all the ingredients by two and the cooking times by one and a half. You need to serve the soufflés as soon as they are cooked because they sink on contact with cold air. This dish is perfect with a tomato-based salad and some nice crusty bread.

1 tbsp. and 1 tsp. butter, at room temperature
1 tbsp. grated Parmesan cheese or bread crumbs
1 tbsp. flour
pinch of salt
1/4 cup milk

1 large egg, separated
3 tbsp. grated Cheddar cheese
1/4 tsp. ground paprika or nutmeg
3 baby tomatoes, quartered

Grease a mug with 1 teaspoon butter. Add the grated Parmesan or bread crumbs, and shake to coat the butter. Put the mug in the freezer while you prepare the soufflé mixture. Melt 1 tablespoon butter in a microwave bowl on HIGH for 30 seconds. Beat in the flour and salt. Stir in the milk and beat until smooth. Cook on HIGH for 20 seconds. Beat again, and cook for another 20 seconds. Add the egg yolk, cheese, and paprika or nutmeg and microwave for 20 seconds. Beat until smooth. Stir in the tomatoes.

In a separate bowl, whisk the egg white until stiff. Fold half into the hot cheese sauce mix, then gently fold in the remaining half. Handle carefully to retain as much air as possible. Pour into the mug. Microwave on LOW for 1 minute, then on MEDIUM for 1 minute. Serve immediately.

Serves 1

variations

quesadilla with tomato, cheese & chili sauce

see base recipe page 61

quesadilla with beans
Replace the tomatoes with 1/4 x 14-ounce can baked beans. Use the hot chili sauce or replace with brown sauce.

zucchini & blue cheese quesadilla
Use 1/4 cup each of Cheddar and blue cheese. Replace the tomato with 1 small zucchini, grated onto a sheet of paper towel and blotted to removed excess liquid. Omit the chili sauce.

quesadilla with peppers
Slice a jalapeño pepper and 1/4 red or green bell pepper. Follow the basic recipe, sprinkling over the jalapeño and pepper slices.

quesadilla with tuna & cheese
Follow the basic recipe, adding 2 tablespoons drained, canned tuna over the cheese with the tomato.

variations

ham, garden pea & pesto linguine

see base recipe page 62

shrimp, garden pea & pesto linguine
Replace the ham with 1/3 cup cooked peeled shrimp.

goat cheese, garden pea & pesto linguine
Replace the ham with 1/4 cup chopped goat cheese.

ham, garden pea & tapenade linguine
Replace the pesto with tapenade and a squeeze of lemon juice.

garden pea & lemon–garlic linguine
Omit the ham, tomatoes, and pesto. While the pasta is cooking, very finely
slice 1/2 garlic clove. Once the pasta and peas are drained, return to the pan,
pour over 1 1/2 tablespoons olive oil and add the garlic. Cook, stirring the
garlic in the oil, for 1 minute. Add 1 tablespoon freshly squeezed lemon juice
and cook for another minute. Season generously with salt and black pepper.

variations

mozzarella & tomato salad

see base recipe page 65

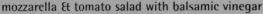

mozzarella & tomato salad with balsamic vinegar
Drizzle about 1/2 teaspoon balsamic vinegar over the finished salad. This is particularly good for adding flavor if you do not have any fresh herbs.

three-colored salad
Cut 1/2 peeled and pitted avocado into thin slices. Add it to the salad, alternating between the tomato and mozzarella slices.

mozzarella & salami
Alternate 6 thin slices of salami between the tomato and mozzarella slices.

corn caprese salad
Heat a small skillet on a medium-high heat. Put 3 tablespoons frozen corn directly in the pan—do not defrost. Cook until the corn is browned all over. Let cool. Make the mozzarella and tomato salad as directed and sprinkle over the corn.

variations

chicken not-pot-noodle

see base recipe page 66

thai curry shrimp noodle soup
Replace the chicken with 1/3 cup small cooked shrimp. Add 1 teaspoon Thai curry paste with the other ingredients.

tofu noodle soup
Replace the chicken with 1/3 cup chopped tofu.

miso beef noodle soup
Replace the chicken with 1 small, thin slice of raw beef, cut into strips. Use 1 packet of instant miso soup mix instead of the bouillon powder or cube. Add 1 small red chile, sliced, with the other ingredients.

peanut butter noodle soup
Add 1 tablespoon peanut butter and 1/4 teaspoon each of white wine vinegar and runny honey with the other ingredients. Be sure to stir well — it will take a while to incorporate. Sprinkle over 1 teaspoon sesame seeds to serve.

turkey & avocado sandwich

see base recipe page 67

warm salmon & avocado sandwich
Broil a 4-ounce piece of salmon fillet for about 3 minutes on each side until just cooked through. Let cool slightly, then use instead of the turkey breast. Eat while still warm.

turkey, avocado & coleslaw sandwich
Spread the bread with butter or low-fat spread instead of cream cheese. Pile 2 tablespoons coleslaw on top of the turkey and omit the cranberry sauce.

turkey & carrot apple sandwich
Combine 1 tablespoon each of grated carrot and apple. Stir in 1 teaspoon mayonnaise and 1/2 teaspoon lemon juice. Use instead of the tomato and cranberry sauce.

turkey & salsa sandwich
Replace the cranberry sauce with 1 tablespoon chunky salsa.

variations

spicy pepperoni french bread pizza

see base recipe page 68

hawaiian french bread pizza
Make the French bread pizza, replacing the pepperoni with 2 slices of ham, torn into small pieces, and 1 pineapple ring from a can, well drained and sliced.

caramelized onion french bread pizza
Melt 1 tablespoon butter or oil in a skillet over a medium heat. Add 1 sliced white onion and cook, stirring occasionally, until clear. Sprinkle over a pinch of sugar and continue to cook until golden brown. This will take about 15 minutes. Meanwhile, construct the French bread pizza as directed in the basic recipe, then replace the pepperoni with the caramelized onion.

french bread pesto pizza
Make the French bread pizza, replacing the tomato purée and herbs with 2 tablespoons pesto. For a vegetarian version, replace pepperoni with sliced peppers.

french bread leftovers pizza
Make the French bread pizza, replacing the pepperoni with leftovers from the refrigerator. A little cooked chicken, ham, tuna, or sausage would be ideal combined with corn, broccoli, mushrooms, peppers, tomatoes, or olives. Use up blue cheese, feta, or goat cheese, too. You need about 6 tablespoons of toppings per slice.

lemon fish

see base recipe page 70

curried fish steaks
Replace the salt and pepper with about 1/2 teaspoon medium curry powder for each fish fillet. Use your hands to rub it into the top of the fish well. Cook and finish as directed, omitting the paprika.

parmesan-crusted fish
After drizzling the fish fillets with lemon juice and zest, sprinkle 1 tablespoon grated Parmesan cheese over the top of the fish. Do not baste. (Unsuitable for microwave cooking.)

baked lemon fish steaks
Preheat the oven to 400°F (200°C). Prepare the fish as directed and put it into an ovenproof dish. Bake, uncovered, for about 8 minutes until opaque, basting half way through the cooking time.

seared tuna or salmon
Prepare your tuna or salmon as for the fish fillets, omitting the lemon juice. Heat a skillet until very hot. Add the olive oil, heat for 20 seconds, then add the fish. Cook for 1 minute only on each side — the middle of the steak will still be pink. Serve with a drizzle of lemon juice, zest and the topping as directed.

variations

power-up roughie

see base recipe page 71

protein power-up roughie
Add 1 beaten egg to the drink. Be sure the egg is fresh. Do not eat uncooked eggs
if you are pregnant or your immune system is compromised. As an alternative, add
1 tablespoon protein powder.

peach ice-cream roughie
Make the roughie, replacing the banana with half a ripe, peeled, and pitted peach and
the yogurt with 1 scoop of soft vanilla ice cream.

chocolate–banana roughie
Make the roughie with 1 banana, chocolate milk (or chocolate soy milk), and 1 scoop of
soft vanilla ice cream.

strawberry–orange roughie
Make the roughie, replacing the banana with 8 large strawberries, and use orange juice
instead of orange and mango juice.

variations

bean & tomato pantry soup

see base recipe page 73

spicy black bean & tomato soup
Add 1 to 2 teaspoons chili powder and 1/2 teaspoon ground cumin to the cooked onions and fry for 1 more minute. Replace the white beans with black beans. Squeeze the juice from 1/2 lime into the finished soup.

bean & smoked bacon soup
Chop 3 slices of smoked bacon into small pieces and fry with the onion.

tomato & roasted pepper soup
Replace the beans with a 12-ounce jar roasted peppers, well drained and chopped. Also add 1 teaspoon sweet or smoked paprika to the ingredients when cooking the soup.

coconut, bean & tomato soup
Make the soup using only 1/2 cup water. To the finished soup add 1/2 cup unsweetened coconut milk. Omit the toppings.

variations

stir-fry shrimp with noodles

see base recipe page 74

stir-fry shrimp italian style
Omit the ginger and soy sauce. Add a pinch of dried basil or oregano with the pak choi.
When the shrimp are cooked, add 1/2 teaspoon tomato purée and 3 tablespoons water.
Heat through and season to taste with salt and pepper.

chili veg stir-fry
Omit the shrimp. Replace the soy sauce with Thai sweet chili sauce and a squeeze of
lemon juice.

chicken stir-fry
Replace the shrimp with 1 small, thinly sliced chicken breast. Stir-fry the chicken with the
chile and garlic for 3 to 4 minutes until it is cooked and white throughout. Remove from
the pan and set aside. Proceed as directed, returning the chicken to the pan when
adding the soy sauce.

stir-fry beef in oyster sauce
Replace the shrimp with 1 thin slice of frying steak cut into thin strips across the grain
(cutting it this way makes the meat tender). Stir-fry the beef with the chile and garlic for
about 2 minutes until it is browned. Remove from the pan and set aside. Proceed as
directed, returning the beef to the pan when the vegetables are cooked. Replace the
soy sauce with bottled oyster sauce.

big mushroom sandwich

see base recipe page 77

creamy mushroom sandwich
Cut the portabello mushroom into slices or use 2 cups sliced chestnut or white mushrooms. Put the oil, vinegar and chili flakes into a small pan with 1 teaspoon butter. Fry the mushrooms for 3 to 4 minutes, turning frequently until tender. Stir in 2 teaspoons sour cream or Greek yogurt. Serve in the toasted bun as directed.

mushroom wrap
Cook the portabello mushroom as directed. Let it cool and cut it into slices. Lay the mushrooms in a row across the bottom of a tortilla. Spread about 2 teaspoons mayonnaise on top of the mushrooms and season with salt and pepper. Top with 4 mozzarella slices and a sliced roasted pepper from a jar. Roll each tortilla tightly, starting at the bottom and tucking in the filling as you roll. Cut in half to serve.

bacon & mushroom breakfast muffin
Prepare the mushroom sandwich as directed. While cooking the mushrooms, fry 2 slices of bacon until crisp. Toast an English muffin. Top with the mushrooms and bacon.

mushroom & cheese sandwich
Broil the mushroom and toast the bun as directed. Put the mushroom on the base of the roll and top with a slice of Cheddar or Swiss-style cheese or 2 tablespoons crumbled blue cheese. Return to the broiler until just melted. Finish the bun as directed.

variations

chicken & black bean tacos

see base recipe page 78

cheese & bean tacos
Omit the chicken. Mix the sauce ingredients in a saucepan and add 1 cup black or kidney beans and 6 tablespoons frozen or canned corn. Bring to a boil, reduce the heat and simmer for 3 minutes. Remove from the heat and add 1/2 cup crumbed feta cheese. Proceed as directed.

ground beef & bean tacos
Do not make the sauce. Instead, stir-fry 8 ounces lean ground beef with the vinegar, chili, cumin, and oregano until evenly browned. Add the black beans and stir-fry to heat through. Season with salt and pepper. Serve as directed.

shrimp & bean tacos
Follow the basic recipe, replacing the chicken with 1 1/2 cups peeled and deveined raw shrimp. (If using cooked shrimp, there is no need to sauté—just add them to the seasoned sauce and heat through.)

very quick ham & corn tacos
Omit the sauce. Combine 1 cup chopped ham and 6 tablespoons canned corn to 1/2 cup prepared mild or spicy salsa. You can heat it through or serve it cold. Proceed as directed.

cheese & tomato soufflé in a mug

see base recipe page 80

cheese & spinach soufflé in a mug
Replace the tomatoes with 10 baby spinach leaves.

corn & tomato soufflé in a mug
Replace the cheese with 3 tablespoons canned corn.

pesto cheese soufflé in a mug
Replace the paprika or nutmeg with 1 teaspoon pesto.

blue cheese & ham soufflé in a mug
Replace the Cheddar cheese with blue cheese and the tomato with
1 tablespoon finely chopped ham.

30 minutes to cook

Everyone needs a repertoire of fuss-free meals that are substantial and satisfying, but easy to prepare. Many of these recipes are simplified versions of more complex ones — they may not be entirely authentic, but they are still very tasty. The magic crust pizza is a brilliant take on the original. Who would think you could make pizza from scratch in just 30 minutes?

spiced carrot & lentil soup

see variations page 109

This hearty vegetarian soup is delicious and satisfying on a cold winter day. Serve with really good crusty bread for an inexpensive meal. Make sure that the pieces of vegetable are not too large or the soup will take longer to cook. If you have a stick blender, you could purée the finished soup.

1 cup dried red lentils
1 quart vegetable bouillon
1 medium onion, chopped
3 large carrots, washed (not peeled)
   and chopped or grated

1 garlic clove, finely chopped
1 tsp. mild or medium curry powder
salt and black pepper
Greek yogurt, to serve

Wash the lentils in a strainer under cold running water until the water runs clear.

Put the lentils and the other ingredients in a large saucepan. Bring to a boil, then simmer for 15 to 20 minutes, until the lentils and carrots are soft. Adjust the seasoning to taste. Purée, if desired, and serve hot with a dollop of Greek yogurt.

Serves 3–4

sweet & sour pork

see variations page 110

The gloopy, red, sticky take-out version of this dish bears no resemblance to this mouth-watering meal, with its crisp, bright vegetable flavors cut with the juicy tanginess of pineapple. It is traditionally served with noodles or rice, but works well cross-culturally with couscous, polenta, stuffed into a pita, or even accompanied by some plain old bread.

8 oz. lean pork steak or tenderloin, trimmed of
    fat and cut into thin strips
1 tsp. grated gingerroot or ginger purée
1/2 tbsp. soy sauce (preferably light soy sauce)
1 tbsp. sunflower oil
1 small onion, cut into 6 wedges
1 small carrot, peeled and thinly sliced on
    the diagonal
1/2 red bell pepper, sliced
4-in. (10-cm.) piece of cucumber, peeled,
    seeded and roughly chopped

1 slice of canned pineapple in natural
    juice, drained, and chopped (reserve
    the drained juice)

sauce
1/4 cup pineapple juice from the can
2 tbsp. ketchup
1 tbsp. vinegar
1/2 tbsp. soy sauce (preferably light)
1/2 tbsp. sugar
1/2 tbsp. cornstarch

Put the sliced pork, ginger, and soy sauce in a small bowl and set aside for about 10 minutes while you prepare the sauce and chop the vegetables.

Put all the sauce ingredients in a separate bowl and mix well. Set aside.

Heat the oil in a wok or heavy skillet over a high heat until hot. Add the pork and stir-fry for 3 to 4 minutes until evenly seared and the center of the meat is no longer pink. Remove from

the pan and keep warm. Toss the onion and carrot into the same pan and stir-fry for 2 minutes. Add the red bell pepper and stir-fry for 2 to 3 minutes until the vegetables are tender-crisp.

Return the pork and any juices to the pan. Give the sauce a quick stir, then add it to the pan. Bring to a boil, then immediately reduce the heat to a simmer. Add the cucumber and pineapple, then continue to simmer for 2 minutes, or until the sauce has thickened.

Serves 2

vegetable & cashew thai green curry

see variations page 111

This creamy vegetarian dish can be gently spicy or quite fierce, depending on your taste or mood. If it is your first time with a particular brand of Thai curry paste, add a little of it first, then add more to taste, because they vary widely in strength! This dish goes well with a portion of sticky jasmine rice but is delicious with any type of rice or noodle. For non-veg and microwaved versions, see the variations on page 111.

1 tbsp. vegetable oil
1 small onion, sliced
4 oz. fresh baby corn
1/2–1 tbsp. Thai green curry paste
14-oz. can low-fat coconut milk
1 medium head of broccoli, broken into florets, stems sliced

4 chestnut or white mushrooms, sliced
1/3 red bell pepper, sliced
1/3 cup unsalted cashew nuts
1 tsp. lime or lemon juice
pinch of salt
pinch of sugar

Heat the oil in a wok or large skillet, then add the onion and baby corn. Stir-fry the mixture for 2 to 3 minutes. Stir in the curry paste and coconut milk. Cover and simmer over a low heat for about 2 minutes. Add the broccoli to the pan and return to a boil. Cover and continue to cook for another 8 minutes, until the broccoli is almost tender.

Toss in the mushrooms and red bell pepper and return to a boil, then simmer for 2 to 3 minutes until the vegetables are tender-crisp. Stir in the cashew nuts and lime juice before serving. Season with salt and sugar, to taste.

Serves 2

penne with bacon & beans

see variations page 112

A reliable meal that always satisfies. Vary the quantities of the ingredients according to your appetite and the contents of your refrigerator. This is not fancy food, but it is tasty and it will fill you up — which is sometimes just what you need.

2 cups dried penne or similar pasta
1/2 tsp. oil
2 slices of bacon, chopped
1/2 small to medium red onion
1 garlic clove, finely chopped
1/2 x 14-oz. can chopped tomatoes

1/4 x 14-oz. can beans (cannellini, black, pinto)
1 tsp. dried basil, oregano or mixed herbs
salt and black pepper
grated Parmesan or Cheddar cheese (optional)

Bring a medium pan of water to a boil and cook the penne for about 10 minutes, or according to package directions. When the pasta is just cooked through, drain it.

Meanwhile, heat the oil in a large skillet and cook the bacon for 2 minutes until it just begins to release its fat. Stir the onion into the bacon and cook for 4 minutes, then add the garlic and cook for 1 minute. Add the canned tomatoes, beans, and dried herbs. Bring to a boil, then reduce the heat and simmer for 5 minutes, stirring occasionally.

Toss the mixture into the drained pasta. Season to taste with salt and black pepper and serve with Parmesan or Cheddar cheese, if desired.

Serves 1

egg-fried rice with shrimp

see variations page 113

If you have frozen shrimp and garden peas in the freezer, then you've got this tasty dish as a cupboard standby. I suggest you cook up enough rice for four people, use some for this recipe and divide the remainder between three plastic bags and freeze as soon as cold. Brown rice is healthier but takes longer to cook, so it is brilliant to have already cooked in the freezer. Remember — all rice needs cooling and freezing quickly otherwise it can cause food poisoning.

2 tsp. vegetable or sunflower oil
1 garlic clove, sliced
1/2 red chile, sliced
1 cup cooked brown or white rice
1/4 cup frozen garden peas
1 egg, beaten

1 cup medium cooked shrimp, shelled and deveined
2 scallions, sliced
2 tsp. soy sauce
chopped fresh cilantro or parsley (optional)

Heat the oil in a wok or skillet and add the garlic and chile. Stir-fry for 20 seconds. Add the rice and toss until very hot, then add the peas and egg and continue to toss until the egg is set. Add the shrimp, scallions, and soy sauce, mix everything together, then stir in the chopped cilantro or parsley, if using.

Serves 1

chicken fajitas

see variations page 114

A Tex-Mex classic. If you want it even spicier, add a few drops of chili sauce. The ingredients can be prepared in advance, then covered and refrigerated in the marinade for up to 12 hours. This recipe serves two, but if you are on your own, eat one portion and make a wrap for lunch with the leftovers. Serve with tortillas (warmed in the microwave) and, for a feast, some good tomato salsa, guacamole, or sour cream.

1 chicken breast, sliced
1/2 red onion, sliced
1/2 green bell pepper, sliced
1/2 red or yellow bell pepper, sliced
1 green chile, sliced (optional)
squeeze of fresh lime juice

marinade
1 garlic clove, finely chopped
1 tsp. ground coriander
1 tsp. paprika (preferably smoked)
1/4 tsp. ground cumin
1 tsp. dried oregano
1 tbsp. olive oil
pinch of salt

Combine all the ingredients for the marinade in a large bowl. Add the sliced chicken, onion, peppers, and chile, if using, and toss to evenly coat everything in the marinade.

Get a wok or large skillet very hot over a high heat. Tip in the contents of the bowl and cook over a high heat using a heatproof wide spatula to keep the contents moving. Continue to stir-fry for 7 to 8 minutes, or until the chicken is just cooked through—if you overcook it, it will become dry. Cut open one of the thickest slices of chicken to check it is done. The vegetables should be tender-crisp. Squeeze over the lime juice, and serve immediately.

Serves 2

magic crust pizza margherita

see variations page 115

Keep some self-rising flour in your cupboard especially for this ingenious recipe, which offers a very simple way of cooking pizza. You can be as creative as you like with the toppings. The ideas on page 115 will get you started.

1 cup Greek yogurt
1 1/4–1 1/2 cups self-rising flour,
   plus more to dust
1/4 tsp. salt
1 tbsp. pesto

3 tbsp. tomato purée
salt and pepper
4 oz. torn mozzarella
1 medium tomato, sliced

Preheat the oven to 450°F (230°C).

Put the yogurt, 1 1/4 cups of the flour and the salt in a bowl and mix with a spoon until combined. Turn out the mixture onto a generously floured worktop and knead for about 5 minutes. Add a little additional flour to help the dough come together, as required. The dough is ready when it is no longer sticky and forms into a stretchy ball of dough.

Using a floured rolling pin, roll and pull the dough into a rough circle about 1/4 inch (5 mm) thick. Don't worry if the shape isn't perfect! Spread the center of the base with the pesto, then with tomato purée, and season with salt and pepper. Distribute the cheese evenly across the surface and top with the tomato slices. Bake for 12 to 15 minutes, or until the crust has browned and the cheese has melted.

Makes 1

salmon & vegetable couscous parcels

see variations page 116

This is a cunning and simple way to cook a one-pot meal with almost no washing up. Be really careful to make well-sealed pockets or the bouillon could pour out and scald you. Alternatively, use a cleaned aluminum dish from a takeout and seal the top with foil instead.

oil or spray oil, to grease
3/4 cup couscous
grated zest and juice of 1 lemon
1 small carrot, grated
1 small zucchini, grated
1 tbsp. chopped fresh or 1 tsp. dried parsley

1 tbsp. olive oil
salt and pepper
1/2 fish bouillon cube
boiling water
2 salmon fillets, 4–5 oz. each

Preheat the oven to 400°F (200°C). Cut 4 sheets of tin foil to 12 x 12 inches (30 x 30 cm). Lay 2 stacked sheets of foil on a work surface, and repeat, to make 2 squares. Grease the center of each square.

Combine the couscous, lemon zest and juice, carrot, zucchini, parsley, and olive oil in a bowl. Season with salt and pepper, to taste. In a heatproof measuring cup, crumble the 1/2 bouillon cube, then pour over 1 cup boiling water and stir to mix. Divide the couscous mixture equally between the two squares of foil. Using your spoon, spread out the couscous slightly, then top with the fish. Bring up the sides of each square of foil and tightly double-fold the top edge where the sides meet. Double-fold one of the open ends of each to form packets. Crimp the edges to form tight seals.

Put the parcels into an ovenproof dish (in case your seals are not tight) with the open ends facing the same direction. Tip the pan to raise up the open ends of each parcel slightly, then carefully pour 1/2 cup hot bouillon into each parcel. Fold over the openings very tightly, leaving room for the steam to circulate inside the packet as the food cooks. Bake for 20 minutes. Remove from the oven and leave to rest for 2 minutes before making a small hole away from you to allow the steam escape, then open the parcel from the top. Eat from the parcel or transfer to a plate.

Serves 2

cheat's chicken satay

see variations page 117

Not one for the purists, but this recipe makes for a quick, simple, and tasty meal. Serve it with rice or rice vermicelli and maybe some stir-fried greens such as pak choi.

1 tbsp. sunflower oil
2 scallions, sliced
1 skinless, boneless chicken breast, cut
    into 1-in. (2.5-cm.) pieces
1/4-1/2 tsp. chili powder
2 tsp. soy sauce

1 tsp. lime juice
1 1/2 tbsp. crunchy peanut butter
1 tbsp. unsweetened shredded coconut
    (optional)
1 tsp. sweet chili sauce or white sugar
1/4 cup water

Heat the oil in a skillet over a medium-high heat and fry the scallions for 2 minutes. Add the chicken and fry for 5 to 6 minutes, or until cooked through and lightly browned. Pierce a piece to check that it is white throughout.

Add the chili powder to the pan and fry for 1 minute. Add the soy sauce, lime juice, peanut butter, coconut (if using), sweet chili sauce or sugar, and water, then simmer for about 3 minutes, adding a little extra water if the mixture becomes too thick. Serve with your preferred side dishes, such as rice and stir-fried greens.

Serves 1

spiced carrot & lentil soup

see base recipe page 95

spicy carrot, lentil & coconut soup
Add 14-ounce can coconut milk and reduce the bouillon to 2 1/2 cups.

spicy lemon, zucchini & lentil soup
Replace the carrots with 3 medium grated zucchini. Add the grated zest and juice
of 1 lemon.

curried parsnip & lentil soup
Replace the carrots with 3 medium parsnips, evenly chopped. Add 2 tablespoons mango
chutney or 1/2 grated apple with the other ingredients.

ham & lentil soup
Use only 1 carrot and add 1 cup diced ham to the soup with the other ingredients. Replace
the curry powder with 1 teaspoon each of French mustard and dried thyme or
mixed herbs. As the ham is salty, you shouldn't need to add salt.

bottom-of-the-refrigerator soup
Replace the carrots with about 2 cups mixed vegetables — any you have left in the
refrigerator (such as beans, carrots, celery, parsnips, garden peas, potato, spinach, squash,
tomatoes, or zucchini).

variations

sweet & sour pork

see base recipe page 96

sweet & sour chicken

Replace the pork with 1 large skinless, boneless chicken breast, thinly sliced.

sweet & sour tofu

Replace the pork with half a block of tofu cut into cubes and tossed in 1 tablespoon cornstarch. Stir-fry until evenly browned and crisped. Return to the pan when the sauce is thickened and serve immediately to retain crispiness.

pork & beansprout stir-fry

Omit the sauce, cucumber and pineapple. Add 1 cup bean sprouts to the wok when the vegetables are just cooked and stir-fry for 1 minute to heat through. While heating, add 1 1/2 tablespoons soy sauce, 1 teaspoon rice vinegar (or 1/2 teaspoon balsamic vinegar), 1/2 teaspoon sugar, and plenty of black pepper. Serve with a drizzle of sesame oil, if available.

very quick pork stir-fry

Omit the sauce and vegetables. Stir-fry the pork as directed. In the wok, stir-fry 1 cup frozen vegetables until just tender-crisp. Add 1 1/2 tablespoons soy sauce, 1/2 tablespoon rice vinegar (or 1 teaspoon balsamic vinegar), and 1 teaspoon each of peanut butter and sugar.

vegetable & cashew thai green curry

see base recipe page 99

thai red curry
Replace the Thai green curry paste with Thai red curry paste. Be aware that the Thai red curry paste is made with red chiles and tends to be hotter than the green one.

shrimp thai green curry
Omit the cashew nuts and add 1 1/2 cups uncooked, peeled and deveined small shrimp and 1/2 teaspoon fish sauce (optional) with the red bell pepper. The shrimp should be opaque at the same time as the vegetables are cooked.

chicken & cashew thai green curry
Cut 1 skinless, boneless chicken breast into thin slices. Add it with the broccoli.

microwave vegetable thai curry
Put 2 cups frozen mixed vegetables into a bowl and stir in 1/2 to 1 tablespoon Thai green or red curry paste and 1 cup coconut milk. Mix well and cover with a plate. Cook on HIGH for 4 to 6 minutes until the vegetables are just cooked. Add the cashews and a squeeze of lime juice. Leave for 1 minute, then serve.

variations

penne with bacon & beans

see base recipe page 100

beans & torn mozzarella on toast
Omit the pasta. Make the bacon and bean sauce and add about 2 ounces torn mozzarella to the finished sauce instead of Parmesan or Cheddar. Serve over toasted sourdough or whole wheat bread.

penne with ham & beans
Omit the bacon. Sauté the onion in 1/2 tablespoon olive oil, then continue to make the sauce in the pan as directed, adding about 1/4 cup chopped ham with the beans.

penne with tuna & corn
Omit the bacon and beans. Sauté the onion in 1/2 tablespoon olive oil, then continue to make the sauce in the pan as directed, adding 1/2 cup tuna chunks, drained, and 4 tablespoons frozen or canned corn with the tomatoes.

penne with beans & sausage
Replace the bacon with 2 sausages. Sauté for about 12 minutes in 1 teaspoon vegetable oil to cook through and crisp, turning occasionally. Remove the sausages from the pan. At this point begin to cook the pasta and make the tomato sauce. Cut the sausages into slices and add to the sauce with the beans.

egg-fried rice with shrimp

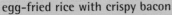

see base recipe page 101

egg-fried rice with crispy bacon
Replace the shrimp with 2 slices of bacon, cut into pieces. Stir-fry for 3 to 4 minutes to crisp, then proceed with the basic recipe.

indian-style egg-fried rice
Hard-boil 2 eggs and cut in half (page 47). Omit the shrimp. Proceed as directed, adding 1/2 teaspoon ginger purée and 1 teaspoon mild curry powder with the chile. When the rice is hot, add the eggs and heat through. Stir in a few drops of vinegar with the soy sauce.

chicken & egg-fried rice
Omit the shrimp and follow the basic recipe. Add 1/3 cup cooked chicken to the hot rice with the scallions.

a side of egg-fried rice
Heat the oil and stir-fry the rice until hot. Add half a beaten egg and continue to cook until the egg is set. Season with salt and pepper. Omit all the other ingredients.

variations

chicken fajitas

see base recipe page 102

beef fajitas
Replace the chicken with 6 ounces skirt or frying steak cut across the grain into 1/2-inch (1-cm.) slices.

beany fajitas
Follow the basic recipe, omitting the chicken. After the vegetables have been cooking for 4 minutes, add 1/2 14-ounce can kidney or black beans, rinsed and drained, and 2 tomatoes, cut into quarters. Heat through and finish as directed.

lemon–cilantro chicken fajitas
Add the juice of 1 lemon, 1 tablespoon chopped fresh cilantro and 1/4 teaspoon runny honey or sugar to the marinade. Proceed as directed. Omit the lime juice and sprinkle more fresh chopped cilantro over the finished dish.

fish fajitas
Replace the chicken with 1 white fish fillet (such as pollock, cod, or haddock). Brush the fish all over with the marinade, cut it into pieces and set aside. Proceed to cook the vegetables as directed. When cooked, transfer to a bowl and keep warm. Add 1 teaspoon oil to the pan and cook the fish for about 2 to 3 minutes on each side until just cooked through. Return the vegetables to the pan and cook for 1 minute.

magic crust pizza margherita

see base recipe page 105

pepper pig pizza
Replace the tomato with 2 ounces sliced pepperoni and 1/3 cup torn sliced ham. Sprinkle over 1/2 teaspoon red chili flakes.

chicken & mushroom pizza
Along with the tomato add 1/4 cup shredded cooked chicken and 2 sliced chestnut mushrooms.

antipasto pizza
Along with the tomato add 1 marinated artichoke, cut into quarters; 1 roasted red bell pepper, sliced; 6 black olives; 10 mushroom slices; and 1 sliced pickle. (Alter the ingredients according to the contents of your jar of antipasto.)

spinach & egg pizza
Omit the pesto. Along with the tomato add 1/4 cup frozen spinach. Distribute the spinach, tomato and mozzarella around the pizza, leaving the center free. Break an egg into the center and bake as directed.

salmon & vegetable couscous parcels

see base recipe page 106

chicken & couscous parcels
Replace the fish with 6 small chicken tenders (mini fillets). Bake for 30 minutes.

moroccan fish parcels
Stir 1 teaspoon harissa paste and 2 tablespoons raisins into the couscous with the other ingredients.

mushroom & lemon couscous parcels
Replace the fish with 2 cups mixed mushrooms (button, chestnut, oyster, and portabello) cleaned, trimmed and cut into 1/2-inch (1 cm.) pieces. Add 1 finely chopped garlic clove to the couscous mixture.

creamy salmon parcels
Season the salmon generously with salt and pepper and put a piece in each parcel. Top with 1 tablespoon each of sour cream or crème fraîche, orange juice, and chopped parsley. Put inside a foil parcel and bake as directed. Omit all the other ingredients.

cheat's chicken satay

see base recipe page 108

chicken satay salad
Make the chicken satay adding 1/4 cup coconut milk to the sauce. Let cool. Make a salad from shredded Chinese cabbage or lettuce and sliced carrot, cucumber, snow peas, and peppers. Pour the cooled chicken and sauce over the salad. Sprinkle over 1 teaspoon toasted sesame seeds.

chicken satay wrap
Make the chicken satay. Let cool. There will be enough for 2 wraps. Lay 2 tortilla wraps on a surface and, in the center, arrange some shredded iceberg lettuce and thinly sliced cucumber. Top with the satay chicken. Fold the wrap to enclose all the ingredients and cut in half.

spaghetti with chicken satay sauce
Make the chicken satay, adding 1/4 cup coconut milk to the sauce. Cook 3 ounces spaghetti in boiling water for 5 minutes, add 1/4 cup frozen garden peas, then return to a boil and cook for 3 to 5 minutes until the pasta is just cooked. Drain the pasta and toss with the chicken satay sauce, then serve immediately.

quick, quick, slow

These recipes can be started off quickly, then left to cook while you do other things. As all the effort is up front, when you return to the kitchen, your meal is ready and waiting for you. Some recipes, like the stew and the tagine, give you quite a long cooking time to play with, while others, such as the cheese & corn bake, give you just enough time for a shower. Most are substantial and don't need much by way of accompaniment—a little rice or bread, maybe, or a green salad.

cheese & corn bake

see variations page 132

The lightness of this dish is balanced by its richness of flavor. You will find that this is a recipe you will return to again and again when there is little else in the cupboard, and you will always be pleased that you did. It works well with both white and whole wheat bread crumbs, which you can grate directly from the loaf—it doesn't have to be super-fresh bread either! This dish is great served with a simple salad.

1/2 small onion, finely chopped
1/2 cup fresh bread crumbs
1/2 cup grated sharp Cheddar cheese
1/2 cup canned or frozen corn

1 egg, beaten
1/2 tsp. French mustard
1 cup milk
generous pinch of salt and pepper

Preheat the oven to 400°F (200°C).

Grease a small, shallow oven dish. Combine all the ingredients in a bowl and pour into the prepared dish. Bake for 40 to 45 minutes, or until set and golden brown on top.

Serves 2

just-like-mom's beef stew

see variations page 133

This is the good old family stew that has been made for generations. If you are in a hurry, you can omit the first stage of pre-browning the meat. This seals and caramelizes the meat, adding flavor, but is not absolutely essential. Big stews improve with time, so it is fine to make this a day ahead and keep it refrigerated until required, or to freeze it in batches for a rainy day. Omit the potatoes and serve with mashed potatoes, if that is your preference.

2 lb. stewing steak, trimmed of visible fat and
    cut into 1 1/2-in. (4-cm.) cubes
salt and pepper
2-3 tbsp. olive or sunflower oil
2 tbsp. balsamic vinegar
1 1/2 cups water
3 tbsp. tomato purée
2 tbsp. all-purpose flour

1 large onion, cut into 1-in. (2.5-cm.) chunks
16 new potatoes, scrubbed
3 medium carrots, cut into 1/2-in.
    (1-cm.) rounds
1 1/2 cups beef bouillon
3 garlic cloves, finely chopped
2 bay leaves
1 tsp. mixed dried herbs

Preheat the oven to 325°F (160°C).

Pat the beef dry with paper towels, then season with salt and pepper.

In a large casserole or heavy oven-proof pot, heat 1 tablespoon oil over a medium-high heat. Brown the meat in two or three batches, turning to brown evenly, cooking for about 5 minutes per batch and adding 1 tablespoon oil for each batch. (If you attempt to sear the meat in one batch, it will not brown.) Transfer the meat to a plate and set aside.

Add the vinegar and about 1/2 cup water to the pan and scrape off all the crusty meaty bits that have stuck to the bottom of the pan (deglazing), as this will add flavor. Add the tomato purée and flour, and stir until smooth. Return the meat to the pan with the rest of the water and all the other ingredients. Bring to a boil.

Cover, transfer to the oven, and cook for 2 to 2 1/2 hours, or until the meat is tender. Remove the bay leaves, taste, and adjust the seasoning as required.

Serves 4 generously

keema curry

see variations page 134

Curry doesn't come any easier or less expensive than this! Adjust the amount of curry powder to taste, and you could add a chile or two as well, if you like your curries hot and spicy. It is a good dish to cook in advance and heat up when you are hungry. Serve with naan bread and some chopped cucumber mixed with yogurt.

1 lb. lean ground beef or lamb
1 onion, finely chopped
1–1 1/2 tbsp. medium curry powder
3 medium potatoes, peeled and diced
3/4 cup beef bouillon

14-oz. can chopped tomatoes
salt and pepper
1/2 cup frozen garden peas
lemon wedge, to serve (optional)

In a large skillet, brown the ground beef or lamb and onion for 5 to 6 minutes over a medium heat (there is no need for oil as the meat will release enough fat of its own). Use a wide spatula or wooden spoon to move the ingredients around in the pan, breaking up the meat into small grains and allowing it to brown evenly. Add the curry powder and potatoes and cook for 1 minute, stirring.

Pour in the bouillon and tomatoes and season with salt and pepper to taste. Bring to a boil, reduce the heat, cover and simmer for 25 minutes, or until the potatoes are cooked. Stir in the peas and cook for another 5 minutes. Serve accompanied by a lemon wedge, if desired.

Serves 3

no-fuss spaghetti with bolognese sauce

see variations page 135

This is a core recipe for ground beef. Every family has its own special twist, so go ahead and add your favorite ingredient. Although, truth be told, this basic version is delicious as it is. There is no need to buy overly expensive ground beef, but avoid the cheapest as it is high in fat. This recipe feeds four people, but you can freeze the sauce in individual portions if you do not need it all and cook the spaghetti as required.

1 medium onion, chopped
1 lb. ground beef
2 garlic cloves, finely chopped
2 tbsp. tomato purée
14-oz. can chopped tomatoes
1 tsp. dried basil

1 tsp. dried oregano
salt and pepper
12 oz. dried spaghetti
1 tbsp. sunflower or olive oil
grated Parmesan cheese, to serve

In a large skillet, brown the onion and ground beef for 5 to 6 minutes (there is no need for oil as the meat will release fat). Use a wide spatula or wooden spoon to move the ingredients around the pan, breaking up the meat into small grains and allowing it to brown evenly. Remove from the heat and tip the pan to allow the fat to drain into one section. Remove the fat with a spoon and discard. You may need to brown the meat in two batches if your pan is not large — overcrowding results in stewed, not browned, meat.

Return the pan to the heat and add the garlic. Cook for 1 minute, then add the tomato purée, tomatoes, basil, and oregano and season with salt and pepper. Reduce the heat and simmer for 30 minutes. When you are ready to eat, bring a pan of water to a boil and add

1 tablespoon oil. Add the spaghetti and allow the long strips of spaghetti to soften into the pan. Stir with a fork to separate the strands and ensure that all are submerged. Cook for about 8 minutes, or until just tender. Drain in a colander and serve with the sauce and grated Parmesan.

Serves 4

panzanella salad

see variations page 136

This is an inspired use of old bread, passed down from Italian peasants, for whom it was born out of necessity. It is best made with full-flavored, slightly soft tomatoes. For the best visual effect, use different varieties and colors of tomatoes. If your bread isn't very dry, put it into a warm oven for ten minutes.

1 1/2 cups ripe tomatoes, chopped
salt
5 oz. good, stale bread (such as ciabatta, sourdough, or French bread)
2 tbsp. balsamic vinegar
1 small red onion, finely sliced
2 roast peppers from a jar, chopped

1/4 cup pitted black olives
1 tsp. capers
1 garlic clove, finely chopped
3 tbsp. olive oil
black pepper
10 sprigs of fresh basil, torn

Put the tomatoes in a bowl, sprinkle with salt, and put them in a colander to drain while you make the salad.

Tear the bread into pieces that are about the same size as the tomatoes and put them into a salad bowl, then moisten with the vinegar. Add the onion, peppers, olives, capers, and garlic.

Squash the tomatoes slightly with the back of a spoon, then add them to the salad ingredients. Dress the salad with olive oil and plenty of black pepper, to taste. Toss to combine, then leave to sit at room temperature for 30 to 60 minutes. Sprinkle over the basil to serve.

Serves 2

meatloaf

see variations page 137

This is a versatile dish that can be served hot with gravy or tomato salsa (page 199), or cold for lunch, or even sliced and used in a sandwich. There are endless variations on this staple recipe, but it is probably best when made with more than one type of meat. If you haven't got a suitable pan, then try the bacon-wrapped variation on page 137.

1 medium zucchini, coarsely grated
1 1/2 lb. ground beef, lamb and/or turkey
3 slices of bread, crumbled
1 egg
2/3 cup milk
1 small onion, finely chopped
4 white or chestnut mushrooms, chopped

1 tbsp. Worcestershire sauce
1 tsp. oregano
1 garlic clove, finely chopped or
    1 tsp. garlic purée
salt and pepper
1/4 cup ketchup

Preheat the oven to 375°F (190°C).

Put the grated zucchini onto 2 paper towels and press out the excess water. Then put it into a mixing bowl with all the other ingredients, except the ketchup. Press the mixture into an ungreased 9 x 5-inch (3-cup) loaf pan, or an ovenproof dish with a similar capacity. Spread the ketchup on top.

Bake for 1 to 1 1/4 hours, or until firm, then turn out onto a serving plate and strain off any excess fat. Leave to stand for 5 minutes before serving with more ketchup or with a fresh tomato salsa.

Serves 4–6

sticky chicken drumsticks

see variations page 138

Chicken drumsticks are economical and, cooked in honey and mustard, are easy to make. (This recipe can be made using chicken thighs, too. There are instructions on how to use ribs and sausages using the same formula in the variations given on page 138.) Serve with a coleslaw or a herby tomato salad. Wrap the leftovers in foil and take them with you for lunch the next day.

4 chicken drumsticks
salt and black pepper
2 tbsp. whole-grain mustard

2 tbsp. runny honey
1 tsp. soy sauce

Preheat the oven to 350°F (175°C).

Put the chicken drumsticks into a baking tray lined with parchment paper. Sprinkle with salt and pepper.

Combine the honey, mustard, and soy sauce in a bowl. Brush the mixture over the chicken.

Bake for 25 to 30 minutes, brushing the chicken with the juices once. Check that the chicken is cooked through by inserting a knife into the thickest part and easing open the flesh to ensure there is no pink showing and the juices are running clear.

Serves 2

spicy chorizo bake

see variations page 139

This dish is oh-so rich and delicious! Serve with a green side salad to balance out all that spicy tomato flavor. To make it slightly less rich, omit the cream. You can prepare the pasta and sauce in advance, then cover and chill until required.

1 dried spicy chorizo, about 10 oz.
2 small red onions, chopped
2 garlic cloves, finely chopped
1 tsp. red chili flakes
2 bay leaves
14-oz. can chopped tomatoes, drained
1/2 cup water
1/4 beef or chicken bouillon cube, crumbled

1/4 nutmeg, freshly grated
1 tsp. dried rosemary, thyme, or mixed herbs
1/4 cup heavy cream
2 1/2 cups pasta (use penne, rigatoni, or orecchietti)
1/2 cup crumbled goat cheese or torn mozzarella cheese

Preheat the oven to 400°F (200°C). Remove the papery casing from the chorizo and crumble by hand or chop into small chunks of about 1/2 inch (1 cm.). This job is a bit messy.

In a large, dry skillet, sauté the sausage meat, stirring until the meat is beginning to crisp and has released plenty of fat. Remove from the heat and tip the pan to allow the fat to drain into one section, then remove it with a spoon and discard.

Add the onion, garlic, chili flakes, and bay leaves to the pan and cook gently for about 5 minutes or until the onions are soft. Add the tomatoes, water, crumbled bouillon cube, nutmeg, and dried herbs and bring to a boil. Remove from the heat and stir in the cream. Meanwhile, cook the pasta in boiling water for 8 to 10 minutes, or until just cooked (it is important not to overcook pasta for baking). Drain the pasta and transfer to a shallow

ovenproof dish. Pour over the sauce and mix. Sprinkle over the cheese. If cooking from hot, bake for 10 to 15 minutes, until bubbling; if cooking from cold, cook for about 30 minutes.

Serves 3

variations

cheese & corn bake

see base recipe page 119

spinach & cheese bake
Omit the corn and replace with 1 small handful of baby spinach leaves, roughly chopped, and add 1 teaspoon dried dill weed, if available. Any remaining spinach could form the basis of your side salad.

roasted pepper & cheese bake
Omit the corn and replace with 1 chopped roasted pepper from a jar. Add 1/2 teaspoon paprika and 1/2 teaspoon mixed herbs.

artichoke & pepper bake
Follow the recipe for the roasted pepper & cheese bake above, but add a roughly chopped marinated artichoke heart and a couple of chopped olives. This is useful for using up a jar of mixed antipasto.

corn & blue cheese bake
Follow the basic recipe, substituting crumbled sharp blue cheese such as Stilton for the grated Cheddar.

variations

just-like-mom's beef stew

see base recipe page 120

beef & beet stew
Use only 1 large carrot. Add 2 medium beets, peeled and cut into 1-inch (2.5-cm.) chunks.
You may also substitute 2/3 cup red wine for the water in this or any other of the beef
stew recipes.

beef & bean stew
Use only 8 potatoes and, 15 minutes before the end of the cooking time, add a 14-ounce
can of drained and rinsed cannellini (white kidney) beans.

beef stew with rice
Omit the potatoes and, 30 minutes before the end of the cooking time, add 1/3 cup
long-grain rice, 1/4 cup raisins, 1/4 cup slivered almonds, and 1 teaspoon sweet
or smoked paprika.

italian beef stew with tomatoes
Add 3/4 cup canned chopped tomatoes with the other ingredients.

variations

keema curry

see base recipe page 123

spinach keema curry
Replace the garden peas with 1 handful of baby spinach leaves and cook until wilted.
Alternatively, add 1/4 cup frozen spinach and cook for 3 minutes.

gingered keema curry
Add 1 teaspoon finely chopped fresh gingerroot (or use 1 teaspoon ginger purée) and
2 finely chopped garlic cloves with the curry powder. Squeeze lemon juice over the finished
curry and garnish generously with chopped fresh cilantro.

cauliflower keema curry
Replace the potatoes with 4 cups medium-sized cauliflower florets. Proceed as directed,
cooking for about 20 minutes, until the cauliflower is tender. Finish as directed.

chicken & potato curry
Follow the basic recipe, using 1 pound diced chicken instead of the ground meat.
Gently cook the onions in 1 tablespoon oil for 5 minutes until soft and clear. Add the
chicken and cook until white all over to seal. Proceed as in the basic recipe.

variations

no-fuss spaghetti with bolognese sauce

see base recipe page 124

fancy spaghetti with bolognese sauce
Chop 4 slices of smoked bacon, add to the oil and cook until crisp. Add the onion, plus
1 stalk of celery, 1 carrot, 1/2 green bell pepper, all finely chopped, and cook for 5 minutes.
Remove from the pan. Brown the beef and add 1/4 cup red wine (optional), bubble for
2 minutes, then add the bacon and vegetables and proceed as directed. Add 4 sliced
mushrooms at the end of the cooking time and cook for another 10 minutes.

sloppy joes
Cook the Bolognese sauce as directed. Using a spoon, pile sloppy meat onto the base of a
toasted, buttered crusty roll and cover with bun tops.

greek lamb stuffed peppers
Replace the ground beef with lamb. Cut 4 bell peppers in half lengthwise and remove the
seeds and membrane. Spoon the meat sauce into the pepper cavities and bake at 350°F
(175°C) for 20 minutes. Sprinkle with crumbled feta cheese and bake for another 10 minutes.

vegetarian spaghetti with bolognese sauce
Replace the beef with vegetarian mince, usually made from soy protein. It is fat- and
cholesterol-free, so is good for weight watching too. Check packet directions for exact
substitution instructions.

variations

panzanella salad

see base recipe page 126

panzanella with anchovies
Add 2 finely chopped anchovies from a can with the olives and capers.

greek bread salad
To the salad, add a 6-inch (15-cm.) piece of cucumber, unpeeled, seeded and chopped, and 1/2 cup cubed feta.

spanish bread salad
Add a 4- to 6-ounce dry chorizo sausage, casing removed and thinly sliced. If you choose uncooked chorizo sausages, sauté first, then cool before slicing.

goat cheese & arugula bread salad
Replace the capers and olives with a handful of arugula leaves and 1/2 cup crumbled goat cheese.

variations

meatloaf

see base recipe page 127

meatloaf with cheesy spinach layer
Prepare the meatloaf as directed and press half the mixture into the pan. Sprinkle over 3/4 cup grated Cheddar cheese and 1 2/3 cup baby spinach leaves. Top with the remaining mixture and proceed as in the basic recipe.

turkey meatloaf with cumin
Use ground turkey only instead of mixed ground meat. Add 1 1/2 teaspoons ground cumin and 2 tablespoons chopped fresh cilantro to the mixture. Proceed as directed.

bacon-wrapped meatloaf
Shape the meat into a rectangular-shaped loaf and put it into a baking sheet that has been lightly greased with olive oil. Spread ketchup on the top of the loaf and arrange 7 to 10 bacon slices on top, tucking the edges underneath. Sprinkle with brown sugar and a pinch of cinnamon. Bake as directed.

quick microwaved meatloaf
Press the meatloaf mixture into a microwave-safe glass or plastic loaf pan, or a dish with a similar capacity. Spread with ketchup. Cook on HIGH for 15 minutes, then allow to stand and finish cooking for 10 minutes before serving.

variations

sticky chicken drumsticks

see base recipe page 129

sticky ribs
Replace the chicken with 1 pound pork ribs. Cover the baking dish with tin foil. Decrease the oven temperature to 325°F (160°C) and cook for 90 minutes, turning and basting twice. Increase the temperature to 400°F (200°C) and cook for 10 minutes. As these take so long to cook, it's economically wise to double the quantities.

sticky sausages
Replace the chicken with 4 good, thick pork sausages. Thin sausages will take a little less time to cook — about 20 minutes.

honey–lemon drumsticks
Replace the mustard with the juice of 1/2 lemon and 1 finely chopped garlic clove.

chipotle–satsuma drumsticks
Omit the sauce ingredients. Replace with the juice of 1 satsuma and 1 to 2 chopped chipotle chiles in adobo sauce.

spicy chorizo bake

see base recipe page 130

sausage ragoût pasta bake
Replace the chorizo with 3 to 6 herby or other well-flavored sausages, depending on size.
There's no need to remove the casings, simply cut them into 1/2-inch (1-cm.) slices and sauté
in 1 tablespoon oil, then proceed as directed.

meatball pasta bake
Replace the chorizo with 12 ounces prepared meatballs. Sauté in the skillet in 1 tablespoon
oil, then proceed as directed.

vegetarian sausage pasta bake
Replace the chorizo with 10 ounces vegetarian sausage. Heat 1 tablespoon oil and sauté
sausages until lightly golden. Remove from the pan, then slice into 1/2-inch (1-cm.) pieces.
Return to the pan with the tomatoes. Proceed as directed.

eat-now chorizo ragoût
After adding the tomatoes and herbs, simmer the sauce for 10 minutes while cooking the
pasta. Stir in the cream and serve over the hot pasta. Omit the cheese.

cooking for a crowd

It's great to be able to cook for friends and family. The recipes in this chapter mostly serve four, but can be easily bulked up to serve eight, or even twelve. They are not difficult to cook and are suitable for a range of occasions. The tagine, ratatouille, or risotto would be good for a supper party; the soup is great to come home to after watching a game; and the low-maintenance baked potato is the perfect comfort food.

pumpkin & prune tagine

see variations page 154

A great vegetarian all-in-one sharing meal. Don't be put off by the word "prune" — after they have been slow-cooked they barely resemble their raw selves and become soft, rich and incredibly sweet. If you are not convinced, use dried apricots, dates, or pears instead.

1 tbsp. sunflower oil
1 large onion, chopped
2 garlic cloves, finely chopped
1 tsp. ground cinnamon
1 tsp. ground cumin
1 tsp. paprika
1 tsp. turmeric (optional)
14-oz. can chopped tomatoes

14-oz. can garbanzo beans, drained
1 1/4 lb. pumpkin, cut into 2-in. (5-cm.) chunks
10 dried prunes, roughly chopped
2 cups vegetable bouillon
1/2 cup bulgur wheat
2 tbsp. yogurt, to serve (optional)

In a large pan, heat 1 tablespoon oil over a medium-high heat until hot. Reduce the heat, add the onion and cook for about 5 minutes until soft. Add the garlic and cook for 1 minute. Add the cinnamon, cumin, paprika, and turmeric and cook for 1 minute.

Add the tomatoes, garbanzo beans, pumpkin, prunes, and bouillon. Bring to a boil, then simmer gently for 15 minutes. (If you don't need to eat immediately, prepare the recipe up to this point, then let cool, refrigerate and continue later.) Stir in the bulgur wheat, cover, then simmer for another 15 minutes until the vegetables are tender, the bulgur wheat is cooked and the liquid has been absorbed. Serve with a dollop of yogurt, if desired.

Serves 4

warming minestrone

see variations page 155

Minestrone is a guaranteed winner—everyone enjoys this wonderful, classic soup. To get the best of the vegetable flavors, sauté them in oil in the order given, which makes them truly luscious.

2 tbsp. extra virgin olive oil
1 large onion, chopped
3 garlic cloves, finely chopped
2 stalks of celery, sliced
1 large carrot, chopped
6 oz. string beans, trimmed and cut
    into 1/2-in. (1-cm.) pieces
3/4 cup shredded cabbage
1 tsp. dried basil

1 tsp. dried oregano
salt and freshly ground pepper
1/4 x 14-oz. can chopped tomatoes
5 cups vegetable or chicken bouillon or
    canned broth
14-oz. can kidney beans, rinsed and drained
3/4 cup small pasta such as orzo
grated Parmesan cheese, to serve (optional)

Heat the oil in a large pan over medium-high heat. Add the onion and cook for about 5 minutes, or until soft. Add the garlic and cook for 1 minute. Add the celery and carrot and cook for 2 minutes. Stir in the string beans and cook for 2 more minutes. Finally, add the cabbage with the basil and oregano, and salt and pepper to taste, then cook for 2 minutes.

Add the chopped tomatoes and the bouillon and bring to a boil. Reduce the heat and simmer for 20 minutes. Stir in the kidney beans and pasta and cook for about 10 minutes until the pasta and vegetables are tender. Adjust the seasoning, if required. Serve in bowls with the Parmesan cheese, if using.

Serves 5–6

oven-baked risotto

see variations page 156

Risotto is cheap, tasty, and filling. The big drawback is that you are tied to the stove as it cooks, but not with this oven-baked version. Serve this dish with oven-baked halved tomatoes and a green salad.

2 tbsp. butter
1 small onion, chopped
1 1/2 cups risotto (Arborio) rice
1 quart hot vegetable bouillon (made from a cube)

1 cup frozen garden peas
1/2 cup chopped ham
grated zest and juice of 1/2 lemon
salt and black pepper

Preheat the oven to 400°F (200°C).

Melt the butter in a casserole or flameproof oven dish. Add the onion and sauté over a medium heat for about 5 minutes, or until soft. Add the rice and then continue to cook for 1 to 2 minutes, stirring, until translucent. Pour over the hot bouillon, add the peas, stir, then bring to a boil. Cover with a tightly fitting lid and bake for 18 to 20 minutes, or until the rice is tender.

Stir through the ham and lemon zest and juice and season to taste with salt and pepper. Cover and allow to rest for 3 minutes before serving.

Serves 4

chili

see variations page 157

Everyone should know how to cook this all-time favorite. It is one of the best recipes for bulking up and it tastes even better when reheated. Serve with rice or warmed tortillas, a bowl of guacamole or a green salad.

1 medium onion, chopped
1 lb. ground beef
2 garlic cloves, finely chopped
2–3 tsp. chili powder
1 tsp. ground cumin
1 green bell pepper, sliced
2 tbsp. tomato purée

14-oz. can chopped tomatoes
1–2 x 14-oz. cans kidney beans
1/2 cup frozen or canned corn
1 tsp. dried oregano
salt and pepper
sour cream, to serve

In a large skillet, brown the onion and ground beef for 5 to 6 minutes (there is no need for oil). Use a wide spatula or wooden spoon to move the ingredients around in the pan, breaking up the meat into small grains and allowing it to brown evenly and release fat. Remove from the heat and tip the pan to allow the fat to drain into one section, then remove with a spoon and discard. Note: You may need to brown the meat in two batches if your pan is not large; overcrowding results in stewed rather than browned and sealed meat.

Return the pan to the heat, add the garlic and cook for 1 minute. Add the chili powder and ground cumin and cook for 1 minute. Toss in the green bell pepper, then cook for another minute. Stir in the tomato purée, tomatoes, kidney beans, corn, and oregano and season with salt and pepper, then simmer for 30 minutes. Serve in bowls topped with sour cream.

Serves 4

baked potatoes with herbed cheese & slaw

see variations page 158

This is comfort food at its most homey. Unless you are lucky enough to have a food processor, cut the cabbage by hand using a very sharp knife and cutting as finely as you can. Grate the carrot. Local greengrocers or market stall holders will often cut you a half or even a quarter of white cabbage.

4 baking potatoes (russet or similar
    floury potato)
olive oil
salt
1/2 cup cream cheese with herbs

coleslaw
2 tbsp. mayonnaise
1 tbsp. lemon juice
1/2 tsp. French mustard
1/4 tsp. white sugar
1/4 tsp. salt
1/4 small white cabbage, finely shredded
1 large or 2 small carrots, grated
1 small onion, finely sliced

Preheat the oven to 400°F (200°C).

To make the slaw, combine the first five ingredients in a serving bowl, then add the cabbage, carrot and onion and toss to evenly coat. Cover and set aside until required.

Scrub the potatoes under running water and pat them dry. You don't need to remove the eyes, but cut away any blemishes. Using a fork, prick eight to twelve deep holes all over each

potato, so that moisture can escape while cooking. Rub the potatoes all over with a little olive oil using your hands, then sprinkle with salt.

Bake the potatoes directly on the oven rack for 1 hour or until the skins feel crisp but the flesh beneath feels soft. (If you're cooking more than four potatoes, you'll need to increase the cooking time by up to 15 minutes.) Serve by cutting a cross in the center of each potato, then, holding it with a kitchen towel to protect from the heat, squeeze all four corners to squash the flesh out a little. Top each potato with a portion of the cream cheese and serve with the slaw.

Serves 4

sausages with cheesy polenta

see variations page 159

Polenta is an excellent staple ingredient. Be sure to buy instant polenta or you will find yourself attached to the stove for 50 minutes! Like pasta, instant polenta is dried and can be kept in the cupboard to use when there is little else on hand. It is simplicity itself to cook and, with a little cheese for flavoring, is delicious. Don't keep it for sausages — it is great in all those situations that call for mashed potatoes.

8 good sausages
1 cup milk
2 cups water
1/4 tsp. salt

1 1/4 cups instant polenta
2 tbsp. butter
1/2 cup grated Cheddar cheese
paprika, to garnish (optional)

Preheat the broiler on a medium-high setting.

Line the broiler pan with tin foil, if you like, to cut down on washing. Broil the sausages for 10 to 12 minutes, turning occasionally, until cooked through. Make a small incision in one sausage to check that it is no longer pink inside.

Put the milk, water, and salt in a small pan and bring to a boil. Slowly pour in the polenta in a thin stream, beating continuously. Stir for 3 to 4 minutes until it thickens and pulls away from the sides of the pan and the polenta is soft. Stir in the butter and cheese. Serve sprinkled with paprika.

Serves 4

ratatouille with pan-seared halloumi

see variations page 160

A ratatouille shouldn't be a dish of exhausted, overheated vegetables. It should retain a freshness that comes from cooking just enough for the flavors to meld. Instead of halloumi, you could top with the lemon fish on page 70.

1 medium eggplant, chopped
salt
1/4 cup olive oil
1 medium onion, chopped
1 garlic clove, finely chopped
1 small red bell pepper, diced
1 small green bell pepper, diced

2 zucchini, sliced
14-oz. can chopped tomatoes
1 tsp. dried oregano or mixed herbs
salt and black pepper
9-oz. package halloumi cheese
juice of 1/2 lemon

Put the eggplant on a plate and sprinkle with salt. Leave to sit for 15 minutes to draw out the bitter liquid. Pat dry with a paper towel.

Heat the olive oil in a large skillet over a medium heat. Add the onion and cook, stirring occasionally, for about 5 minutes until soft and lightly golden. Add the prepared eggplant and garlic and continue to cook, stirring occasionally, for about 5 minutes until the eggplant is partially cooked. Add the peppers and zucchini and cook for an additional 5 minutes. Add the tomatoes, dried oregano or herbs, and season with salt and pepper to taste. Bring to a boil, reduce the heat, then simmer for 5 to 10 minutes, or until the vegetables are tender.

Cut the cheese into eight slices. About 5 minutes before the vegetables are cooked, heat a non-stick skillet and sauté the halloumi slices for 2 minutes on each side — they should have just a little golden brownness to them. Serve the ratatouille with a little lemon juice squeezed over and topped with the halloumi slices.

Serves 3–4

real chili burgers

see variations page 161

There is always the temptation to buy bargain-basement burgers for reasons of both time and economy. However, if you want to impress, make your own — they are simple to prepare and the reward exceeds the effort. Do not buy very lean ground beef. The fat is essential to bind the burger together and keep it whole.

1 tbsp. sunflower oil, plus extra for brushing
4 burger buns
1 large tomato, thinly sliced
shredded iceberg lettuce
mayonnaise
ketchup

burgers
1 lb. good quality ground beef
1 small onion, very finely chopped
1 garlic clove, finely chopped
2 tsp. ground cumin
2 tbsp. tomato purée
2 tbsp. sweet chili sauce
1 tsp. French mustard
salt and pepper

Mix together the burger ingredients with your hands. Then, shape into four burgers, brush with a little oil and chill for 20 minutes. Heat the oil in a large skillet and sear the burgers over a medium-high heat until well browned on both sides. Reduce the heat and cook for 4 to 8 minutes on each side until cooked to your liking; keep warm.

Cut the burger buns in half and cook them, cut-sides down, in the hot pan so they soak up the delicious juices and become lightly toasted. Layer the buns with the burgers, tomato, and lettuce, adding mayonnaise and ketchup, if desired.

Makes 4

variations

pumpkin & prune tagine

see base recipe page 141

lamb & prune tagine
Once the spices have been cooked, add 1 pound lean cubed lamb, stir to coat in the spices and brown. Add the tomatoes, bouillon, and prunes. Bring to a boil, cover and gently simmer for 1 hour. Add the garbanzo beans and 8 ounces diced pumpkin, and cook for 15 minutes. Proceed with the bulgur as directed.

chicken & prune tagine
Once the spices have been cooked, add 4 chicken thighs, stir to coat in the spices and brown. Add the tomatoes, bouillon and prunes. Bring to a boil, cover and gently simmer for 30 minutes. Add the garbanzo beans and 8 ounces diced pumpkin, and cook for 15 minutes. Proceed with the bulgur as directed.

sweet potato & prune tagine
Replace the pumpkin with 1 pound peeled sweet potato, cut into 2-inch (5-cm.) chunks.

butternut squash & apricot tagine
Replace the pumpkin with 1 butternut squash, peeled, seeded and cut into 2-inch (5-cm.) pieces. Replace the prunes with 10 dried apricots, cut in half.

warming minestrone

see base recipe page 142

winter vegetable stew
Reduce the bouillon from 5 cups to 2 1/2 cups.

ham & garden pea minestrone
Omit the string beans and cabbage. Add 1 cup lean diced ham with the tomatoes and 1 cup frozen garden peas with the pasta.

tomato & basil soup
Replace the kidney beans with white beans and omit the cabbage and pasta. Replace the dried herbs with 2 tablespoons pesto. Add 1/4 cup tomato purée with the chopped tomatoes.

mexican vegetable soup
Omit the basil. Add 1 teaspoon each chili powder, ground cumin, and ground cinnamon with the garlic. Garnish the finished soup generously with some chopped fresh cilantro and sour cream.

variations

oven-baked risotto

see base recipe page 144

mushroom & lemon risotto
Omit the peas and ham. Before cooking the onion, cook 1 cup sliced mushrooms in
2 tablespoons butter. When soft, transfer to a plate, add the butter and onions as in the
basic recipe and proceed as directed, adding the cooked mushrooms with the lemon.

cheese & tomato risotto
Replace the peas with 12 halved cherry tomatoes. Replace the ham with 1 cup grated
Cheddar cheese or 1/2 cup grated Parmesan cheese. Omit the lemon.

spinach & garden pea risotto
When adding the peas and bouillon, stir in 4 cups shredded fresh or chopped frozen spinach.
Replace the lemon juice with 1/4 cup grated Parmesan cheese. Omit the ham.

lemon–shrimp risotto
Add 1/2 to 1 teaspoon red chili flakes with the bouillon. Replace the ham with 1 1/2 cups
small cooked shrimp and heat through. (If using frozen shrimp, stir them into the risotto
after 15 minutes of cooking time to heat through.)

chili

see base recipe page 145

chorizo chili
Follow the basic instructions, using only 12 ounces ground beef and add 8 ounces skinned, crumbled chorizo.

vegetarian chili
Follow the basic instructions, omitting the beef. When adding the green bell pepper, also add 2 chopped carrots, 2 chopped medium potatoes and half a medium butternut squash, chopped. Cook for 3 minutes, then proceed as directed.

chili burritos
For each burrito, spoon chili onto the center of a tortilla, and sprinkle with 2 tablespoons grated Cheddar cheese. Fold the top and bottom edges over the filling, then fold in the sides over the filling to enclose it. Repeat as required. Put the burritos, seam-side down, on a greased baking tray. Broil the burritos about 6 inches (15 cm.) from the heat until crisp and golden brown.

tex-mex shepherd's pie
Boil 1 1/2 pounds potatoes until tender. Mash with 1/4 cup milk and 2 tablespoons butter, then season with salt and pepper. Put the chili in a baking dish, top with the mashed potato and sprinkle with 1/4 cup grated Cheddar cheese. Bake at 350°F (175°C) for 20 to 25 minutes, or until golden brown.

variations

baked potatoes with herbed cheese & slaw

see base recipe page 146

baked potato tuna melt

Scoop out the insides of the baked potatoes, keeping the skins intact. Mash the potato flesh with 1/4 cup milk and 2 tablespoons butter. Add a 5-ounce can drained tuna, 2 chopped scallions and 1 cup grated Cheddar cheese to the potato mixture; season and mix well. Pile back into the potato skins. Bake for another 15 minutes.

baked potatoes with baked beans & cheese

Omit the cream cheese. Heat a 14-ounce can baked beans and use 1/4 cup grated Cheddar cheese to sprinkle over the beans.

baked sweet potato with sour cream & slaw

Prepare sweet potatoes as instructed for the potatoes, but put them on a baking tray lined with tin foil. Bake for 50 to 60 minutes. Proceed as directed, substituting sour cream mixed with 2 chopped scallions for the herbed cream cheese.

microwaved baked potatoes

Wash the potatoes as directed. Cut a wedge out of each potato that is 1/8 inch (3 mm.) wide and 1 inch (2.5 cm.) deep (to prevent the potatoes exploding in the microwave). Put the potatoes on a microwave-safe plate and cook on HIGH, uncovered, for 6 minutes, then turn over and cook for 4 to 8 minutes, or until a fork goes through the centers. Leave to rest for 5 minutes. (If cooking 1 potato, cook for only 3 minutes, turn and cook for another 2 to 3 minutes.)

sausages with cheesy polenta

see base recipe page 149

pork chops with soft polenta
Cook the polenta as directed. Replace the sausages with 4 x 1/2-inch (1-cm.) thick pork steaks or pork chops. Brush with oil and season with salt, pepper, and a pinch of dried mixed herbs. Broil for about 5 minutes on the first side, turn, baste with pan juices and repeat for the second side. Check it is done as for the sausages.

cheesy polenta with mushrooms
Cook the polenta as directed. Prepare the mushroom sauce as for the creamy mushroom sandwich (page 91) and serve with the polenta. Omit the sausages.

polenta slices
Cook the polenta as directed. Pour into a greased 8 x 10-inch (20 x 25-cm.) or similar sized dish and smooth the surface. Let cool, then chill in the refrigerator to set. Cut into pieces and sauté these in a skillet in 2 tablespoons oil or butter over a medium-high heat for 4 minutes on each side until golden.

spicy polenta
Cook the polenta as directed, adding 1 small red chile, seeded and finely chopped, 1 teaspoon mixed dried herbs, and 1/2 teaspoon garlic purée. Use as soft polenta or make into slices following the instructions above.

variations

ratatouille with pan-seared halloumi

see base recipe page 150

ratatouille with kidney beans
Add a 14-ounce can kidney beans, rinsed and drained, with the tomatoes.

ratatouille wraps
Use leftover ratatouille to make wraps. Spoon ratatouille down the center of a tortilla and wrap up over the filling. For a fancier version, spread the tortilla with tapenade (olive paste) before filling.

curried eggplant and peppers
After cooking the onions, add 1 to 2 tablespoons medium curry powder, to taste, and 1 teaspoon ginger purée and cook for 1 minute, stirring. Proceed as directed. Squeeze 1/4 lemon into the finished dish. Indian paneer cheese could be used as a substitute for the halloumi.

ratatouille bake
Once the tomatoes and herbs are added to the vegetables, transfer to an ovenproof dish and add 2 1/2 cups cooked pasta (about 1 1/4 cups dry pasta). Top with 1 cup fresh bread crumbs mixed with 1/4 cup grated Cheddar cheese. Bake at 350°F (175°C) for 20 minutes until the top is golden. Omit the halloumi.

real chili burgers

see base recipe page 153

real classic burger
Make the sweet chili burger omitting the cumin, tomato purée, sweet chili sauce, and mustard. Add 1/4 teaspoon Worcestershire sauce instead.

blue cheese burger
Prepare the meat for the real classic burger above, but shape into eight thin, 4-inch (10-cm.) wide patties. Mound 1 1/2 tablespoons crumbled blue cheese (or other preferred cheese) on each of four patties, leaving a border. Cover each with one of the remaining patties. Press the edges tightly together to enclose. Cook as directed.

real meatballs
Prepare the meat as directed either for the sweet chili burger or the real classic burger, above. Add 1 small beaten egg and 1/2 cup fresh bread crumbs. Mix well. Using wet hands, shape into 1 1/2-inch (4-cm.) balls. Cook in a skillet as directed, turning frequently; they will take about 10 minutes. Cook in batches, if required.

vegan burger
Mix 3/4 cup dry TVP (textured vegetable protein) with 3/4 cup boiling water and leave to stand for 10 minutes. Finely chop 1 small onion, 1 small carrot, 1 stalk of celery, and 1 garlic clove, and sweat them in 1 tablespoon oil in a skillet until just soft. Let cool, then add to the TVP. Flavor and proceed as directed. Use vegan mayo.

cooking to impress

With this collection of fail-safe recipes, you'll soon find you have a reputation for being a great cook. There are a couple of appetizers and a selection of entrées, some are economical and a few require you to spend a little bit more. Spaghetti carbonara is always a popular dish and couldn't be easier to prepare as it requires almost no cooking, while the roast vegetable tart is a show-stopper and will delight vegetarians and meat eaters alike. For fish lovers, you could serve shrimp and coconut chowder followed by the excellent fishcakes.

shrimp & coconut chowder

see variations page 178

This is an impressive soup that is cooked in under ten minutes. Thai curry paste varies hugely by brand, so be sure to add a little to start with and build up the flavor, until it is to your taste.

14-oz. can unsweetened coconut milk
1 cup fish bouillon
1 jalapeño pepper, seeded and thinly sliced
1/2–1 tbsp. Thai green curry paste
1/4 tsp. sugar
1/4 cup water

1 1/3 cups shelled and deveined, medium, raw shrimp
2 scallions, thinly sliced
1/4 cup chopped fresh basil
1/4 cup chopped fresh cilantro
4 lime wedges

In a large pan, combine the coconut milk with the fish bouillon, sliced jalapeño, curry paste, sugar, and water, and bring to a boil. Simmer for 3 minutes. Add the shrimp and scallions and cook for about 2 minutes, or until the shrimp are just white throughout. Stir the basil and cilantro into the soup and serve with lime wedges.

Serves 2–3

bruschetta with pesto & sundried tomatoes

see variations page 179

Everyone loves these tasty morsels as an appetizer and they make an excellent canapé to serve with drinks on any occasion. They are easy to make in bulk, too.

8 slices of French bread or ciabatta
1 garlic clove, halved
8 tsp. olive oil
6-oz. jar of pesto

5-oz. jar of sundried tomatoes in oil, halved if large
fresh basil leaves

Preheat the broiler on a high setting.

Rub one side of each slice of bread with the cut side of the garlic clove, to flavor. Drizzle the outside edge of each slice with 1 teaspoon olive oil. Put the bread under the broiler and toast lightly on each side.

Spread the pesto over each of the slices of toasted bread and top with sundried tomatoes and basil leaves.

Serves 4

carnivore's sharing board

see variations page 180

Sharing boards are popular in many restaurants and provide a sociable, informal start to a meal or a casual evening in with friends. Deli counters offer many options, so take the ones suggested here as a starting point. Look for foods with a range of colors and textures and take a few minutes to fold salami in half or arrange the ham in rolls to look good. Choose an attractive loaf of bread to serve on the side.

8–12 oz. selected cold cuts, such as Parma
    ham, salami, mortadella, roast beef,
    smoked chicken, and smoked sausage
1 tbsp. grainy mustard
1/2 cup coleslaw (page 146)
3/4 cup olives
8 cherry tomatoes
8 slices of ciabatta, French bread or
    sourdough bread

dipping sauce
1/4 cup good olive oil
1 tbsp. balsamic vinegar
1/2 garlic clove, finely chopped or
    1/2 tsp. garlic purée
1/2 tsp. dried basil or oregano
salt and black pepper

Arrange the meats and the spoonful of mustard attractively on a cutting board or serving plate alongside the coleslaw and olives in bowls. Garnish with the tomatoes.

Combine all the ingredients for the dipping sauce in a bowl and place this on the board or plate with the meat.

Serves 4

pork medallions with lemon & parsley

see variations page 181

The thin slices of pork tenderloin cook through in the time it takes to brown them, so this is a very quick and easy recipe, which belies the sophistication of the finished meal. Fresh parsley is essential in this recipe — don't try to substitute dried. Serve with some buttered petite potatoes and some steamed string beans.

8–10 oz. pork tenderloin
salt and black pepper
2 tbsp. olive oil
1/2 cup white wine

juice of 1/2 lemon
1 tbsp. chopped fresh parsley
2 lemon wedges, to serve

To make it easier to handle, freeze the tenderloin for 20 minutes. Cut it into 1/3-inch- (8-mm.) thick slices. Put these between 2 sheets of plastic wrap and beat gently with a rolling pin or a skillet until about half their original thickness. Season with salt and pepper.

Heat half the oil in a large skillet over a medium heat. Add sufficient pork pieces to fill the skillet without overcrowding, then sauté for about 2 to 3 minutes on each side until evenly browned. Remove from the pan, keep warm, and repeat with another batch, adding more oil as necessary. Once browned, add the wine to the empty pan, cook until reduced by about half, then add the lemon juice and parsley. Arrange the meat on warmed plates and spoon over the sauce (there isn't a great deal but it is delicious). Serve with lemon wedges.

Serves 2

spaghetti carbonara

see variations page 182

This is a sophisticated pasta dish that is made in the time it takes to cook the spaghetti. It does contain semi-raw eggs, which means that you shouldn't serve it to anyone with a compromised immune system or anyone who is pregnant. However, the rest of us love its creamy texture punctuated by the saltiness of the bacon. If you want to be authentic, use Italian pancetta, otherwise, regular bacon is fine. Serve with a tomato salad.

6 oz. spaghetti
1 tsp. sunflower oil
6 thin slices of bacon (preferably smoked or pancetta)
1/4 cup heavy cream

1 egg
1 egg yolk
1/3 cup grated Parmesan cheese
black pepper, to serve

Bring a large pan of water to a boil. Add the pasta and cook for about 10 minutes, or as directed on the packet, until the pasta is just done (al dente). Meanwhile, put the oil in a skillet and spread it over the base of the pan. Add the bacon and sauté for about 3 minutes on each side until crisp. Drain on paper towels and, when cool enough to handle, cut into small pieces. While the bacon is cooking, in a small bowl, beat together the cream, egg, egg yolk, and 1/4 cup grated Parmesan cheese.

Drain the cooked spaghetti and immediately return it to the hot pan (do not return it to the heat). Stir in the beaten egg mixture and bacon. The hot pasta will heat and thicken the sauce. Serve immediately, garnished with the remaining Parmesan and lots of black pepper.

Serves 2

steak with basil-garlic butter

see variations page 183

Sometimes, the old favorites are the best. This one is quick to cook and always delicious. For best results, remove your steaks from the packaging and put them on a plate in the refrigerator 2 hours before you start cooking, then remove the plate from the refrigerator 30 minutes before cooking and allow the meat to come up to room temperature.

2 lean sirloin or beef fillet steaks, about
    7–8 oz. each
salt

basil-garlic butter
2 tbsp. salted butter, softened
2 tbsp. chopped fresh basil
1 garlic clove, finely chopped
pinch of grated lemon zest
black pepper

Preheat the broiler to high. Line the broiler pan with tin foil.

In a small bowl, stir together the butter, chopped basil, garlic, lemon zest, and a good grinding of pepper.

Trim the steaks of all visible fat, then place on the lined broiler pan and season with salt and pepper. Cook about 3 inches (7.5 cm.) away from the heat source for 1 1/2 to 4 minutes on each side until done to your liking. Leave to rest in a warm place for 5 minutes before serving. This is essential as it allows the meat to relax and become more tender. Top each steak with a spoonful of the basil-garlic butter.

Serves 2

How to cook a steak

Timings are based on a sirloin steak with a thickness of about 3/4 inch (2 cm.). Cooking times vary depending on the type and thickness of steak, and the heat intensity of the broiler or pan.

Blue: 1 minute on each side.

Rare: 1 1/2 minutes on each side.

Medium rare: 2 minutes on each side.

Medium: 2 1/4 minutes on each side.

Medium–well done: 2 1/2-3 minutes on each side.

Well done: 4 minutes on each side.

tuna fish cakes

see variations page 184

If you're entertaining when money is tight, this is the recipe for you. There are variations using fresh white fish or salmon and shrimp if you want a different take on the idea. Panko bread crumbs are suggested as these produce a light and crisp crust and resist soaking up fat, but regular dry bread crumbs would be fine, too. These fish cakes go well with chunky salsa (page 199) or mango salsa (page 208).

1 1/4 lb. potatoes or sweet potatoes, peeled
    and chopped
12-oz. can tuna in water, drained
2 scallions, chopped
1/2 tsp. chili flakes
grated zest and juice of 1/4 lemon

1 egg
freshly ground black pepper
1 cup panko bread crumbs
3 tbsp. olive oil
1 lemon, cut into wedges, to serve

Cook the potatoes or sweet potatoes in a pan of simmering water for 20 minutes. Drain well and mash. Flake the tuna and add to the potatoes with the scallions, chili flakes, lemon zest and juice, and the egg. Season with black pepper and mix well.

Using wet hands, divide the mixture into eight equal portions and shape into patties. Put the bread crumbs on a plate and lightly press the fish cakes in the crumbs until coated on all sides. Heat 2 tablespoons oil in a large skillet over a moderate heat. Sauté the fish cakes until golden on both sides. If you need to cook in batches, add the remaining oil when cooking the second batch. Serve with lemon wedges.

Serves 4

fusion chicken salad

see variations page 185

A simple salad is enlivened by a sweet, tangy dressing that completely transforms it into something magical. Rotisserie chicken pieces are great for this recipe. If you want it to have more Asian flavors, use shredded pak choi instead of mixed salad greens.

salad
1/2 cup slivered almonds
2/3 cup chopped cooked chicken
2 cups mixed salad greens
1 small carrot, grated
1/2 red bell pepper, sliced
3 scallions, sliced
fresh parsley or cilantro

dressing
1 1/2 tbsp. lime juice
1 tbsp. honey
1 tbsp. Thai fish sauce
2 tsp. sesame oil
1 tsp. soy sauce
2 tsp. finely grated gingerroot or ginger purée
1/2–1 red chile, seeded and finely chopped,
    or 1/2 tsp. red chili flakes
1 garlic clove, finely chopped

Toast the slivered almonds in a hot, dry skillet until lightly colored. Transfer to a plate to cool. In a salad bowl toss together the remaining salad ingredients.

Put all the dressing ingredients in a small jar, screw on the lid and shake until combined. Alternatively, combine the dressing ingredients in a small bowl. When you are ready to eat, pour the dressing over the salad, toss gently, then serve immediately garnished with the toasted almonds.

Serves 2

roast vegetable & feta tart

see variations page 186

A dish of roasted vegetables is a wonderful thing. It can go with simple cooked meat or chicken as a side dish; it can form the basis of a frittata or a salad; or you can serve it with couscous for a vegetarian main dish. Here we have piled the roasted vegetables into a simple tart case for a very impressive-looking entrée.

1 fennel bulb, chopped
1 medium zucchini, chopped
8 oz. cherry tomatoes
1 small red or yellow bell pepper, thickly sliced
1 small red onion, cut into wedges
1 tsp. dried mixed herbs

salt and pepper
2 tbsp. olive oil
1 puff pastry sheet, thawed
1 egg beaten with 1 tbsp. water
2 tbsp. pesto
1/2 cup crumbled feta cheese

Preheat the oven to 375°F (190°C). Arrange the vegetables in a baking dish without overcrowding. Sprinkle over the herbs and salt and pepper, then toss lightly with the oil, coating the vegetables evenly. Roast the vegetables for 30 to 40 minutes, turning halfway through the cooking time. The vegetables should be tender and golden brown. Turn out onto a plate to cool.

Line a baking sheet with parchment paper. Unfold the pastry sheet on a lightly floured surface. Roll the pastry into a 13 x 11-inch (33 x 28-cm.) rectangle. Transfer the pastry to the baking sheet and brush the edges with the beaten egg. Fold over the edges 1/2 inch (1 cm.) on all sides and press with a fork to form a rim. Prick the base of the pastry all over with a fork. Refrigerate for 30 minutes. Preheat the oven to 400°F (200°C). Bake for 10 minutes, then use a spatula to carefully press down the puffed center of the tart to form a shell.

Spread the pesto across the surface of the pastry. Arrange the vegetables over the top, then sprinkle with the feta cheese. Bake for about 10 minutes, or until the pastry is golden brown and the cheese has melted. Serve hot or at room temperature.

Serves 4

roast chicken & potato dinner

see variations page 187

There are times when the need for this homey comfort food is overwhelming. Serve the roast chicken, potatoes, and nuggets of soft garlic with your favorite vegetables.

10 garlic cloves, unpeeled
3 lb. (medium) chicken
1 lemon, halved
2 onions, quartered
2 tbsp. olive oil

salt and black pepper
1 lb. petite potatoes, halved
1 tsp. dried mixed herbs
1 tbsp. flour
3 1/2 cups good chicken bouillon

Preheat the oven to 375°F (190°C). Peel 2 garlic cloves, and bruise them by applying pressure with the flat side of a knife. Use the cloves to stuff the chicken cavity, along with with 2 lemon halves and 4 onion quarters. Put the chicken into a large roasting pan. Using your hands, rub half the olive oil all over the chicken and season with salt and pepper. Arrange the potatoes and the remaining onion quarters and unpeeled garlic around the chicken, sprinkle with herbs, and drizzle with the remaining oil, tossing the potatoes to coat.

Bake for about 1 hour and 20 minutes, basting the chicken with the juices and turning the potatoes twice. To check that the chicken is done, pierce the thickest part of the thigh with a skewer and press gently — the juices should run clear. Alternatively, a meat thermometer should register 165°F (74°C). Allow to sit for 15 minutes before carving.

For the gravy, spoon out any visible fat from the roasting pan, then put the pan on the stove over a low heat. Stir in the flour and cook for 1 minute. Slowly add the bouillon, then,

stirring and scraping up the brown bits on the base of the pan, bring to a boil. Continue to boil, reducing the liquid until it is dark and syrupy. Taste and adjust the seasoning. Pour through a strainer into a warmed pitcher.

Serves 4

variations

shrimp & coconut chowder

see base recipe page 163

coconut–fish chowder
Replace the shrimp with 1 pound pollock, cod or other white fish, cut crosswise into 2-inch-(5-cm.) wide pieces. Increase the cooking time to 5 to 6 minutes, or until the fish is cooked through.

coconut–corn chowder
Add 1 medium-large potato, diced, with the coconut milk. Replace the shrimp with 1 cup frozen or canned corn and use vegetable or chicken bouillon. Increase the cooking time to about 10 minutes, until the corn and potatoes are tender.

old fashioned shrimp chowder
Replace the coconut milk with 2 cups whole milk and the curry paste and sugar with a dash of Worcestershire sauce. Add 1 medium-large potato, diced, with the fish bouillon, then add 1 cup frozen or canned corn with the shrimp. Increase the cooking time to about 10 minutes, or until the potatoes are tender. Use 6 tablespoons chopped fresh parsley instead of cilantro and basil.

coconut–chicken chowder
Make the basic recipe but replace the fish bouillon with chicken bouillon and the shrimp with 2/3 cup chopped cooked chicken. Add 1 medium-large potato, diced, with the coconut milk and 1 cup frozen or canned corn with the chicken. Increase the cooking time to about 10 minutes, or until the corn and potatoes are tender.

bruschetta with pesto & sundried tomatoes

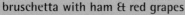

see base recipe page 164

bruschetta with ham & red grapes
Follow the basic recipe, replacing the pesto with 1 thin slice of smoked ham or Parma ham on each side of bread and the tomato with halved red grapes. Omit the basil.

bruschetta with pâté & olives
Follow the basic recipe, replacing the pesto with your favorite pâté and the tomatoes with sliced olives.

bruschetta with pesto, tomato & mozzarella
Follow the basic recipe, replacing the sundried tomato with slices of mozzarella cheese topped with slices of ripe tomato. Garnish with the basil.

bruschetta with pesto & goat cheese
Follow the basic recipe, replacing the tomatoes with slices of goat cheese sprinkled with pepper and topped with the basil.

variations

carnivore's sharing board

see base recipe page 167

fisherman's sharing board
Replace the cold cuts with deli fish such as smoked salmon, smoked trout, anchovies, cooked shrimp, or seafood pâté. Serve with a side of lemon mayonnaise made from 1/4 cup good mayonnaise seasoned with 1/2 tablespoon lemon juice. If you have capers, a few of these are good for garnishing.

vegetarian sharing board
Replace the cold cuts with antipasto such as charbroiled artichokes, roasted red and yellow bell peppers, mixed mushrooms, sweet peppers, sundried tomatoes, and sliced mozzarella cheese.

cheese sharing board
Replace the cold cuts with a range of cheeses such as a soft herb and garlic cheese, a blue cheese, a smoked cheese, a cheese with fruit, a goat cheese, and a good sheep cheese.

tapas sharing board
Replace the cold cuts with a selection of Spanish goodies such as sliced chorizo, cubes of Manchego cheese, deli-bought cheese-stuffed peppers, cooked shrimp on a skewer with a small wedge of orange, toasted almonds, and small wedges of cantaloupe melon.

pork medallions with lemon & parsley

see base recipe page 168

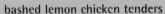

bashed lemon chicken tenders
Replace the pork with chicken tenders, sliced into 1-inch (2.5-cm.) pieces and pounded as for the pork.

pork medallions with mushrooms
Once the pork is cooked, add 1 tablespoon each of butter and olive oil to the skillet and cook 1 1/2 cups sliced mushrooms, 1 finely chopped garlic clove and 1/2 teaspoon dried thyme until the mushrooms are tender. Add the wine and finish as directed.

pork medallions with orange chipotle
Replace the wine and lemon juice with 3/4 cup orange or tangerine juice and 1 to 2 tablespoons chopped chipotle in adobo sauce, to taste.

pork medallions with caramelized onions
Before cooking the pork, heat 1 tablespoon each of butter and olive oil in the skillet and cook 1 large sliced onion over a moderate heat for about 5 minutes, until soft and clear, then add salt and pepper and 1 teaspoon sugar. Continue to cook, stirring frequently, for about 20 minutes until golden brown. Remove from the pan and cook the pork. Serve the pork on a bed of onions topped with the sauce.

spaghetti carbonara

see base recipe page 169

spaghetti with salmon carbonara
Replace the bacon with 1 cup smoked salmon trimmings. The salmon does not need cooking, just add it to the hot pasta.

spaghetti carbonara with lemon & chilli
Add the grated zest of 1/2 lemon and 1/2 teaspoon red chili flakes to the egg–cream mixture.

spaghetti carbonara with garlic zucchini
Increase the sunflower oil to 1 tablespoon and sauté 1 sliced zucchini and 1 finely chopped garlic clove with the bacon. If cooking for vegetarians, omit the bacon and add grated lemon zest and chili flakes, as above.

spaghetti carbonara with asparagus & walnuts
Cook 1 cup asparagus tips in the boiling water for about 3 minutes, until tender-crisp. Drain with a slotted spoon and set aside. Cook the spaghetti in the same water. Omit the bacon and toast 1/2 cup walnuts in the hot skillet without oil for about 2 minutes, then sprinkle with a little sea salt. Proceed as directed.

steak with basil-garlic butter

see base recipe page 170

steak with blue cheese butter
Make the butter by mixing together 2 tablespoons soft butter, 1 tablespoon crumbled blue cheese, 1/2 garlic clove, finely chopped, and 1/2 tablespoon chopped fresh parsley (or 1/2 teaspoon dried parsley).

steak with herbed grilled tomatoes
Cut 2 ripe tomatoes in half and season with salt and pepper. Put tomatoes, cut-sides down, on a broiler pan alongside the steak and cook for 3 minutes. Turn over, drizzle with a little olive oil and a pinch of dried mixed herbs, and cook for another 3 minutes. Serve with the steak.

steak with balsamic marinated mushrooms
Clean 2 portobello mushrooms and trim the stems. Marinate in a mixture of 2 tablespoons olive oil, 1 garlic clove, finely chopped, and 2 tablespoons balsamic vinegar for 1 hour. Broil alongside the steak for about 10 minutes until cooked through.

pan-fried steaks
Heat 1 tablespoon olive oil in a skillet over a moderate heat – the pan must be really hot. Add the steak and cook, using timings given for broiled steak (page 171), turning halfway through. Crisp the fat on the edges by tipping the steak up on its side before finishing cooking. Rest as instructed.

variations

tuna fish cakes

see base recipe page 172

fishcakes
Cook 12 ounces white fish as directed on page 70. You can choose inexpensive fish
for this recipe or the meaty tails and trimmings of larger fish, such as cod and halibut,
which are often sold at bargain prices. Flake the cooked fish, removing skin and bones,
and proceed as directed.

salmon fishcakes with capers
Replace the tuna with 10 ounces canned pink salmon and add 1 teaspoon drained capers to
the fishcake mixture.

tuna & shrimp cakes
Use a 4-ounce can of shrimp and reduce the tuna, fish or salmon to 6 ounces.

sardine fishcakes
Use 2 x 4-ounce cans drained sardines (there's no need to remove the soft bones) and
replace the chili flakes with 1 teaspoon French mustard.

fusion chicken salad

see base recipe page 173

fusion lamb salad
Pan fry an 8-ounce lamb steak in a skillet over a moderate to high heat for 8 to 10 minutes, or until cooked. Shred the lamb, then add it to the salad while still slightly warm.

fusion tofu salad
Cook a packet of tofu as directed on page 110. Leave to cool, then add to the salad instead of the chicken.

fusion jumbo shrimp salad
Replace the chicken with 12 cooked jumbo shrimp.

chicken avocado salad with lime–honey dressing
Add a sliced avocado to the salad. Make the dressing from 2 tablespoons each of lime juice and olive oil, 1 tablespoon honey, 1 garlic clove, finely chopped, 1 teaspoon French mustard, and a pinch each of cumin, salt, and black pepper.

variations

roast vegetable & feta tart

see base recipe page 174

roast vegetable & bean tart
Proceed as directed but mash the contents of a 14-ounce can white beans, rinsed and drained, with the pesto and spread over the base of tart shell.

roast vegetable omelet
Make the omelet following the instructions on page 27. Fill with 1/4 cup roasted vegetables.

roast vegetable pasta
Cook 3 cups pasta. Toss the roasted vegetables with 2 tablespoons balsamic vinegar and mix into the pasta with 2 tablespoons of the pasta cooking water to moisten. Top with crumbled feta.

simply plum tart
Omit the vegetables and pesto. Prepare the tart case as directed. Halve and stone 3 cups plums, then cut into slices. Arrange in the pre-cooked pastry shell, sprinkle with 1/4 cup superfine sugar and 1 teaspoon ground cinnamon and bake as directed.

roast chicken & potato dinner

see base recipe page 176

roast lamb dinner
Replace the chicken with a 3–4-pound leg of lamb. Rub the meat with oil and season as for the chicken. Put the onions into the pan with the potatoes; omit the lemon. Roast at 325°F (160°C) for 25 minutes per pound, plus 25 minutes extra, to yield a medium-cooked roast. Use lamb or beef bouillon for the gravy.

roast beef dinner
Replace the chicken with 2-pound top round and bottom round beef. Rub the meat with oil and season as for the chicken. Put the onions into the pan with the potatoes; omit the lemon. Roast at 425°F (220°C) for 20 minutes, then reduce temperature to 375°F (190°C) and cook for 30 minutes for rare, 40 minutes for medium, or 50 minutes for well done. Make the gravy with beef bouillon.

roast chicken with mixed vegetables
Replace the potatoes with 1 1/2 pounds mixed root vegetables, such as whole baby carrot, chunks of rutabaga, chunks of celery root, whole shallots, and a few small potatoes.

chicken & artichoke bake
Buy or prepare chicken in joints. Put them into a baking dish with the potatoes, onions, and whole garlic and 1 jar of drained artichokes. Squeeze over the juice from the lemon and add the olive oil, dried herbs and salt and pepper to taste. Bake at 375°F (190°C) for 45 minutes, or until the chicken is cooked though. Omit the gravy.

late-night fixes

Coming home after a long day or a night out, having

not eaten for hours, can present a dilemma. Often, a

bowl of cereal just won't cut it and you need something

substantial and tasty that's quick to cook—and

you have only cupboard ingredients to fall back on.

The speedy recipes in this chapter are ideal in these

circumstances. Try the tuna melt toastie or fish finger

sandwich if you are on your own, or if there is a group

of you try the cowboy casserole or home-baked tortilla

chips and salsa.

tuna melt toastie

see variations page 202

The perfect standby, this toastie can be served on rye bread or sourdough — but late in the evening, any bread will do. No bread? See the variations to turn this recipe into a tasty pasta sauce.

2 slices of bread
2 tbsp. ketchup
2 tbsp. mayonnaise
5-oz. can tuna, drained

1/4 cup canned corn, drained
1 tsp. paprika
1/4 cup grated Cheddar cheese

Preheat the broiler on a high setting.

Toast the bread on 1 side only. Meanwhile, put all other ingredients, apart from the cheese, in a bowl and mix well.

Spread the tuna mix onto the untoasted sides of the bread, ensuring the mixture covers the bread. Sprinkle the grated cheese on top. Broil the toasties until the cheese melts and turns slightly brown. Cut in half and serve.

Serves 1

nutty banana sandwich

see variations page 203

Okay, maybe this isn't the most fancy recipe in the world, but if you are hungry and there is nothing else... Anyway, it was much loved by Elvis, apparently. See the variations for his favorite version (with bacon).

1 small ripe banana
2 slices of white or whole wheat bread

2 tbsp. peanut butter (preferably smooth)
2 tbsp. butter

Slice the banana.

Lightly toast the bread, then spread the peanut butter on 1 piece and top with the sliced banana; sandwich together.

Heat the butter in a skillet, then cook the sandwich, turning once, until each side is golden-brown.

Transfer to a plate, cut the sandwich in half and serve.

Serves 1

one-pot mac & cheese

see variations page 204

This is a clever variation on the classic. Instead of cooking the macaroni and making the cheese sauce, you cook the macaroni in the milk and the starches from the pasta thicken the milk into a smooth sauce. Add cheese and you're done!

2 cups large elbow macaroni
2 cups low-fat milk, plus
    extra if required
1/4 tsp. salt

1 tbsp. butter
1 tsp. French mustard
1 1/4 cups grated Cheddar cheese
ground black pepper

Put the raw elbow macaroni in a colander and quickly rinse under water, then drain. Transfer to a medium pan with the milk, salt, butter, and mustard. Slowly bring the mixture to a simmer over a medium heat, stirring frequently. You need to watch carefully or the milk will boil over. Reduce the heat to low and cook the macaroni slowly in the milk, stirring from time to time.

After 15 to 20 minutes the macaroni will be soft and the milk, thickened. If the mixture becomes too thick, add a little extra milk — the amount will vary depending on the brand and cooking time of the pasta.

Stir in the cheese and remove from the heat. Put the lid on the pan and leave to sit for 5 minutes to allow the macaroni to plump up and absorb any excess milk. Adjust the salt to taste and add plenty of black pepper.

Serves 2 generously

crunchy fish finger sandwich

see variations page 205

Always a winner, this nostalgic dish is now frequently found on menus in trendy diners. It works best with good soft white bread or a good-quality white bread roll. If two fish fingers look skimpy on the slice of bread, cook a couple more to fit.

2–3 fish fingers
1 tbsp. butter or spread

2 slices of white bread or 1 white roll
ketchup or mayonnaise

Preheat the broiler on a high setting.

Broil the fish fingers until crisp and golden brown on each side, following the manufacturer's instructions (usually about 5 minutes per side).

Meanwhile, butter the bread slices. Spread a little ketchup or mayonnaise over one slice and top with the cooked fish fingers. Add more ketchup or mayonnaise over the top of the fish fingers and sandwich together with the other slice of bread. Press down gently and cut in half. Eat immediately.

Serves 1

ultimate sausage & bacon crusty roll

see variations page 206

Some people may think that this is breakfast food, but the dish comes into its own late at night when you are really hungry and need a big-tasting protein and carbohydrate boost. Don't eat this every day because that wouldn't be good for you, but as an occasional fix, you can't beat it.

1 tbsp. oil
2 small sausages
2 slices of bacon
1 large crusty roll

1 tbsp. butter or spread
1/2 tsp. French mustard
ketchup

Heat the oil in a skillet over a medium heat and cook the sausages for 3 minutes. Add the bacon and continue to cook, turning occasionally, until the bacon is crisp and the sausages are nicely browned and cooked through. Make a small incision into each sausage to check that it is cooked.

Meanwhile, cut the roll in half and spread with the butter. Spread the base of the roll with the mustard. Cut the sausages in half lengthwise and arrange them on the base. Top with the bacon and ketchup. This sandwich is best eaten hot.

Serves 1

swiss cheese sandwich

see variations page 207

Comfort food at its finest, this sandwich is hot, creamy, and cheesy. If you want to make a meal of it, serve with some green salad leaves and a few baby tomatoes, dressed with a little balsamic vinegar.

2 thick slices of bread
about 2 tbsp. butter
1/2 cup grated Swiss cheese (use Gruyère
   or Emmental)

1 egg
3 tbsp. milk
salt and pepper

Use about half the butter to spread on the bread. Top with the cheese, and sandwich together.

Beat the egg with the milk in a dish that's large enough to contain the sandwich. Season with salt and pepper. Lay the sandwich in the eggy mixture and leave for 5 minutes. Turn the sandwich over and repeat. By this stage, most of the eggy mixture will have been absorbed.

Heat the remaining butter in a skillet over a medium heat. Add the sandwich and cook until it has a dark golden-brown color, then turn and cook the second side, by which time the cheese in the sandwich should have melted, too.

Serves 1

baked tortilla chips & chunky salsa

see variations page 208

This is a great sharing dish, which will keep you and your friends going while you put the world to rights. There are a selection of alternative dips in the variations section.

4 large flour tortillas (plain or with cilantro and garlic)

chunky salsa
3 large tomatoes, deseeded and chopped
1 small red onion, finely chopped

1 garlic clove, finely chopped
handful of fresh cilantro, chopped
1 jalapeño pepper, finely chopped
juice of 1 lime
pinch of ground cumin
salt and black pepper

Preheat the oven to 325°F (160°C).

Using kitchen scissors or a sharp knife, cut each tortilla into eight wedges. Place these on a cookie sheet without overlapping them and bake for 10 to 15 minutes until they are crisp and slightly golden at the edges.

Meanwhile, make the salsa by combining all the ingredients together in a bowl, then adjust the seasoning to taste. Serve with the hot tortilla chips.

Serves 4

cowboy beans with hot dogs

see variations page 209

Here's another one of those handy cupboard standby recipes that cooks in next to no time. Serve in bowls with crusty bread to mop up the yummy juices.

1 tbsp. sunflower oil
1 small red onion, chopped
2 garlic cloves, finely chopped, or
    2 tsp. garlic purée
4-in. (10-cm.) piece of dry chorizo, sliced
1/2–1 tsp. red chili flakes

1/2 x 14-oz. can chopped tomatoes
14-oz. can baked beans
4 canned or chilled hot dogs, cut into
    3/4-in. (2-cm.) slices
black pepper

Heat the oil in a medium-sized pan over a moderate heat, add the onion and cook for about 3 minutes. Add the garlic and cook for another minute, then add the chorizo slices and cook for another 4 to 5 minutes, or until the chorizo has released some of its oils. Add the chili flakes, tomatoes, and beans and cook for 5 minutes. Add the hot dogs and cook for 2 minutes to heat through. Season with pepper to taste.

Serves 2

variations

tuna melt toastie

see base recipe page 189

sicilian tuna melt
Add to the tuna mixture 4 quartered black olives, 1 tablespoon raisins, and 1 teaspoon capers.

tuna pickle melt
Add 2 tablespoons chopped dill pickles and 1 tablespoon finely chopped onion to the tuna mixture.

tuna melt pasta
Cook 3/4 cup pasta in boiling water until just tender. To the tuna mixture, add 1/4 cup sour cream or milk. Stir the mixture into the hot pasta and sprinkle over the cheese.

tuna melt stuffed peppers
Cut a red or green bell pepper in half lengthwise and remove the seeds and membranes. Spoon the tuna mixture into the pepper halves, sprinkle with the cheese, and bake at 350°F (175°C) for 20 minutes.

nutty banana sandwich

see base recipe page 190

nutty banana & bacon sandwich
Cook 2 slices of bacon in the skillet until crisp. Remove and drain on paper towels, then crumble and put on top of the banana. Proceed as directed, using only 1 tablespoon butter added to the bacon fat to cook the sandwich.

chocolate banana on toast
Replace the peanut butter with Nutella or another chocolate nut spread, or you can spread the Nutella on top of the peanut butter if you prefer.

nutty banana roughie
Mash the small banana to a really smooth paste with a fork. Combine with 2 tablespoons smooth peanut butter and 1 tablespoon honey. Stir in 1/2 cup yogurt and use the fork to thoroughly mix together. Transfer to a glass. Pour in sufficient milk (about 1/2 cup) to make a thick drink. If you have a blender, blend all the ingredients together and pour into a glass. Omit the bread and butter.

healthy nutty bananas
Slice 1 big banana in half lengthwise. Combine the peanut butter with 1 tablespoon each of honey and tahini. Spread over the banana. Sprinkle with dried cranberries and mixed seeds. Omit the bread and butter.

variations

one-pot mac & cheese

see base recipe page 193

mac & cheese with cauliflower
While the mac & cheese are cooking, steam the florets from half a medium cauliflower until tender. Stir into the finished mac & cheese before leaving it to rest.

jalapeño & black bean mac & cheese
Stir 1/2 x 14-ounce can of black beans, rinsed and drained, and 2 sliced jalapeño peppers into the finished mac & cheese before leaving it to rest.

mac & cheese with tomatoes
Stir 2 medium chopped tomatoes (preferably skinned) into the finished mac & cheese before leaving to rest.

mac & cheese with crispy bacon
While the mac & cheese are cooking, cook 4 slices of bacon until crisp. Break them into large chunks and serve over the finished mac & cheese.

variations

crunchy fish finger sandwich

see base recipe page 194

upmarket fish sandwich
Replace the ketchup or mayonnaise with tartar sauce. Lay thin slices of tomato and avocado on top of the fish fingers and finish with a squeeze of lemon.

fish finger & dill pickle sandwich
Lay sliced dill pickles over the ketchup or mayonnaise on the first bread slice, then top with the fish fingers.

fish finger & cheese sandwich
Lay slices of mozzarella or Cheddar cheese on top of the ketchup or mayonnaise on the first bread slice. Broil to melt the cheese, then top with the fish fingers.

chicken nugget sandwich
Replace the fish fingers with sufficient cooked chicken nuggets to cover the slice of bread. (Cook them according to the manufacturer's directions.) Proceed as directed.

variations

ultimate sausage & bacon crusty roll

see base recipe page 196

bacon & egg sandwich
After the bacon and sausages are cooked, remove from the pan and keep warm. Fry an egg in the same pan, then add it to the bun over the sausages. And remember that eating runny egg in a bun is a messy business.

sausage & fried onion crusty roll
Omit the bacon. Cook the sausages as directed, remove them from the pan, and keep warm. Drain off excess fat and add 1 tablespoon butter. Once melted, add 1 small sliced onion and a pinch of dried oregano. Sauté the onion until soft and beginning to brown at the edges. Make the sandwich as directed, topping the sausages with the fried onions.

herby sausage sandwich
Omit the bacon and mustard. Cook the sausage & fried onion crusty roll, as above, using herbed or paprika sausages and adding 1/4 sliced red or green bell pepper to the onion. Also add 1 tablespoon ketchup, a few drops of chili sauce, and a pinch of basil.

sausage & sauerkraut roll
Make the sausage & fried onion crusty roll above, using Polish sausage and adding 2 tablespoons prepared sauerkraut to the onion. Also add 1/2 teaspoon sugar, and 1/4 teaspoon caraway seeds, if available.

swiss cheese sandwich

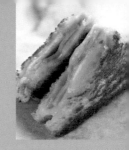

see base recipe page 197

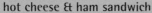

hot cheese & ham sandwich
Prepare the basic recipe, laying a slice of ham on the bread under the cheese.

simple fried cheese sandwich
Omit the egg and milk. Make the cheese sandwich without buttering the bread. Generously spread butter on the outside of 1 side of the sandwich and put it in a hot skillet with the buttered side facing downward. When golden, carefully spread butter on the other side of the sandwich, turn, then fry the second side until golden.

hot cheese & tomato sandwich
Prepare the basic recipe using thin slices of mozzarella cheese topped with slices of tomato. Either dip the sandwich in the egg mixture for Swiss-style sandwich, or cook as above for a simple fried sandwich.

hot cheese & relish sandwich
Prepare the basic recipe, spreading the cheese filling with 1 tablespoon cranberry sauce or fruit-based chutney.

variations

baked tortilla chips & chunky salsa

see base recipe page 199

guacamole
Roughly mash the flesh from 1 large ripe avocado. Combine it with 1 large diced tomato, 1 chopped scallion, 1 small finely chopped garlic clove, and the juice of 1 lime. Add a little chili sauce for a spicy guacamole. Season with salt and pepper and sprinkle with paprika to serve.

mango salsa
Combine the chopped flesh of 1 firm, ripe mango, 1/2 small chopped red onion, 1/2 small red chile, seeded and chopped, the grated zest and juice of 1 lime, a pinch of salt and 1 tablespoon chopped fresh cilantro.

black bean salsa
Make the tomato salsa as directed, adding 1/2 x 14-ounce can black beans, rinsed and drained, with the other ingredients.

red hot salsa
Make the tomato salsa as directed but increase the number of jalapeños to 4. Add 1 to 2 tablespoons chili sauce, to taste. This is good with a side of sour cream.

cowboy beans with hot dogs

see base recipe page 200

vegan cowboy beans
Use vegan sausages instead of meat-based hot dogs. Alternatively, use a packet of falafels in place of the sausages.

cowboy bean & hot dog casserole
Prepare as directed and put the mixture into an ovenproof dish. At the same time, peel and slice 2 medium-large potatoes. Cook in boiling water for 5 minutes and drain. Top the casserole with potato slices, brush with a little olive oil and bake at 350°F (175°C) for about 20 minutes until the top is golden and the potatoes are tender. This dish can be prepared ahead of time and baked when needed.

sausage & beans with leeks
Make the cowboy casserole as directed but use 2 sliced leeks instead of onions and replace the hot dogs with good-quality cooked sausages.

chicken, bean & chorizo casserole
Make the cowboy casserole as directed but use 2/3 cup diced cooked chicken or 2 cooked chicken legs instead of the hot dogs.

on the side

Many of the dishes in the book would be enhanced
by a little something extra on the side. This chapter
gives you a few ideas on how to use potatoes,
rice and grains to make a meal more satisfying. It
is amazing how delicious a simple potato can be
when boiled and crushed with a few herbs, or oven-
baked with some spices. There are also a few simple
side salads and vegetable suggestions, and the
ubiquitous potato salad is always a great standby.

spiced oven wedges

see variations page 225

These are always delicious served as an accompaniment or even on their own as a snack. Cumin and paprika work brilliantly together, but other spice combinations — such as creole spice mix, jerk spice mix, or curry powder — are excellent, too. Use your imagination and what you have in the cupboard. For vegans, serve with plain soy yogurt.

2 tbsp. olive oil
1/4 tsp. paprika
1/4 tsp. ground cumin
salt and pepper

2 baking potatoes (about 8 oz. each)
1/2 cup sour cream, to serve
snipped fresh chives (optional)

Preheat the oven to 400°F (200°C).

Using a large baking sheet, mix the oil with the paprika, cumin, and a little salt and pepper. Cut each potato into eight wedges and toss in the spiced oil to coat.

Bake for 25 to 30 minutes, turning once, until evenly crisp and browned. Serve with a side of sour cream and garnished with snipped chives, if available.

Serves 2

greek salad

see variations page 226

This salad goes with just about anything and makes a change from the tired old lettuce and sliced tomato salads that appear almost everywhere. Choose the ripest tomatoes you can find and dress with the olive oil at the last minute to let the tangy tomato juices flow through the salad.

2 large ripe tomatoes, cut into chunks
1/3 cucumber, deseeded and cut into chunks
1/2 small red onion, very thinly sliced
1 tsp. dried oregano
salt

3 tbsp. olive oil
1 tsp. lemon juice
black pepper
1 cup feta cheese, crumbled
8 Greek olives, pitted

In a bowl, combine the tomatoes, cucumber, onion and oregano. Sprinkle with salt to taste and leave to sit for at least 10 minutes (or up to 2 hours) so that the salt can draw out the natural juices from the tomato and cucumber.

Drizzle with the olive oil and lemon juice, and sprinkle over pepper to taste. Toss the feta cheese and olives over the salad.

Serves 2

italian-style broccoli

see variations page 227

Broccoli is one of those vegetables that most people will eat, but there is a tendency to cook it to death so that it is way too soft and soggy, and tastes of cooking water. Here is a lovely way to cook it and retain its flavor. It goes well with almost everything — add a dash of soy sauce and it is good to go with an Asian dish, or a teaspoonful of garam masala to turn it into a curry, or add some cooked chicken or fried tofu cubes and you have an entrée. Note: If you're using frozen broccoli, omit the first step and toss it in the oil for a few minutes to cook.

1 1/2 cups fresh broccoli, cut into 2-in.
   (5-cm.) pieces
1 tbsp. olive oil
2 garlic cloves, sliced lengthwise in half

pinch of red chili flakes
2 tsp. lemon juice
salt

Put the broccoli in a microwave-safe bowl with about 2 tablespoons water — there's no need to be too accurate. Cover (a plate will do) and cook on HIGH for 2 minutes. Stir to rotate the broccoli pieces, then cook for another 1 to 2 minutes until tender-crisp. To cook conventionally, put the broccoli in a steamer basket in a small saucepan over 1 inch (2.5 cm.) water. Bring to a boil. Cover and steam for 5 to 7 minutes, or until tender-crisp.

Heat the oil in a skillet. Cook the garlic and chili flakes for 1 to 2 minutes until golden brown. Remove from the pan with a slotted spoon and discard. Add the lemon juice and a pinch of salt to the flavored oil and pour it over the broccoli. Toss to coat, then serve.

Serves 2

potato salad

see variations page 228

This is a delicious creamy potato salad with some optional extras — if you were brought up on dill pickles in your salad, go ahead and use them, along with anything else your family favors. If you haven't got sour cream, then use all mayonnaise or Greek yogurt instead.

1 1/2 lb. waxy potatoes such as Charlotte
1 tbsp. cider vinegar or white wine vinegar
pinch of salt
3 scallions, sliced
1/4 cup chopped fresh herbs, (parsley, chives, dill weed or cilantro)
2 stalks of celery, finely chopped (optional)

1/4 cup finely chopped dill pickles or gherkins (optional)
3 tbsp. sour cream or crème fraîche
3 tbsp. mayonnaise
1–2 tsp. French or whole-grain mustard
freshly ground black pepper, to taste

Put the potatoes in a pan of salted water, and bring to a boil. Reduce the heat and simmer for about 20 minutes until just cooked. Drain, leave until cool enough to handle, then peel the potatoes.

Chop the peeled potatoes into bite-size chunks, then put them in a large bowl. Sprinkle the vinegar over the potatoes and season lightly with salt. Toss in the scallions and fresh herbs, plus the celery and pickles, if using. Gently stir through the sour cream, mayonnaise, and mustard, and season to taste with black pepper. Let cool completely, then refrigerate until required, although it is best served at room temperature.

Serves 4 generously

string beans & bacon vinaigrette

see variations page 229

String beans are a popular vegetable to eat on the side. This vinaigrette livens up their taste and turns them into something quite special. As a bonus it works hot or at room temperature.

8 oz. string beans, trimmed
2 slices of bacon, cut into 1/2-in. (1-cm.) pieces
1 scallion, sliced
1/2 tbsp. cider vinegar or balsamic vinegar

1/2 tbsp. whole-grain mustard
1/2 tbsp. olive oil
salt and pepper

Bring a large pan of water to a boil. Add the string beans and cook for 5 to 6 minutes, or until just tender. Drain and transfer to a serving bowl and keep warm.

Meanwhile, in a medium skillet, cook the bacon over a medium heat for 6 to 8 minutes until crisp.

Discard all but 1/2 tablespoon of the bacon drippings from the skillet and return the pan to the heat. Add the scallions and cook for 1 minute. Stir in the vinegar, mustard, and oil and season to taste with salt and pepper. Add the mixture to the string beans, along with the bacon, and toss to combine.

Serves 2

seedy couscous

see variations page 230

Nothing could be simpler or easier than cooking couscous. Serve hot with a tagine, broiled meat, chicken, fish, or stew, or cold as a salad. If serving cold, add the scallions and herbs once the couscous has cooled.

1 1/4 cups couscous
1/2 vegetable or chicken bouillon cube
3 1/2 cups boiling water
1/4 cup mixed seeds
2 scallions, sliced

1/4 cup chopped fresh mint, parsley
  and/or cilantro
1 1/2 tbsp. olive oil
juice of 1/2 lemon

Put the couscous in a heatproof bowl. Dissolve the bouillon cube in the boiling water, pour the bouillon over the couscous and stir well. Cover the bowl with a damp kitchen towel and leave for 5 minutes. The couscous should be soft. Fluff it with a fork.

Meanwhile, toast the mixed seeds in a small skillet until just beginning to brown. Toss into the couscous with the scallion, herbs, olive oil and lemon juice and serve hot or warm.

Serves 4

black beans & rice

see variations page 231

Beans and rice make a staple meal in cultures throughout the world. This is a good dish to have on its own, but it makes a tasty accompaniment too. Use whatever beans you have on hand and substitute brown rice, if you like, but remember it takes longer to cook and you will need a little extra liquid, too. In some places, such as Cuba, hot pepper sauce, slices of mango, and wedges of lime are served on the side.

1 tbsp. olive oil
1 small onion, chopped
1 garlic clove, finely chopped, or
    1 tsp. garlic purée
1/3 cup rice
1/2 tsp. ground cumin
pinch of chili powder

3/4 cup vegetable bouillon, preferably
    low-salt
1/2 tsp. dried oregano
1/2 x 14-oz. can black beans, rinsed
    and drained
2 medium tomatoes, chopped
salt and black pepper

Heat the oil in a medium-sized pan over a medium heat. Add the onion and cook for 5 minutes until soft and clear. Add the garlic and cook for 1 minute. Stir in the rice, cumin, and chili, then cook for another 2 minutes until the grains of rice are translucent.

Pour in the vegetable bouillon and oregano. Bring to a boil, reduce the heat, and simmer for about 20 minutes, or until the rice is tender. Add the black beans and tomatoes, heat through, and season to taste with salt and black pepper.

Serves 2

dhal with spinach

see variations page 232

A versatile side that goes well with any curried dish or vegetable dish and provides protein for a vegetarian meal. It is great, too, with rice or naan bread as an inexpensive supper. It freezes well, so bag up any leftovers. If you don't have coconut milk, don't worry, just substitute water.

1 cup red lentils
1 cup coconut milk
2 cups cold water
3/4 tsp. ground turmeric
1 tsp. ground cumin
1/2 tsp. salt

2 tbsp. sunflower oil
1 small onion, thinly sliced
1 2/3 cups baby spinach or 1/4 cup frozen
    spinach leaves
2 tbsp. chopped fresh cilantro or parsley
    (optional)

Wash the lentils under cold running water, then put them in a pan with the coconut milk and water and bring to a boil. Skim off any scum with a spoon, then add the turmeric, cumin, and salt. Reduce the heat and simmer, uncovered, for about 15 minutes, stirring occasionally, until the lentils have broken down and the dhal resembles porridge in texture. If the mixture gets too thick, add a little more water.

Meanwhile, heat the oil in a skillet over a medium heat. Add the onion and sauté for 7 to 8 minutes, or until golden brown and just beginning to scorch at the edges. Stir into the cooked dhal along with the spinach and leave to sit for 5 minutes until the spinach is wilted and the flavors combined. Serve sprinkled with chopped cilantro or parsley, if using.

Serves 3 as a side, 2 as a main

herby crushed potatoes

see variations page 233

Boiled potatoes can look a bit uninspired. However, half crush them with a few herbs and some butter and they are transformed into quite a trendy side dish. Serve with any meat or fish, or with broiled tomatoes topped with a fried egg for a simple supper.

1 lb. waxy potatoes such as Charlotte
2 tbsp. butter or olive oil
2 tbsp. snipped fresh chives

salt
paprika, to garnish (optional)

Wash the potatoes, but do not peel them. Put them in a medium-sized pan, cover with cold water and bring to a boil over a medium-high heat. Reduce the heat to a simmer and cook for about 10 to 15 minutes, or until tender. Strain and return to the pan.

Add the butter or olive oil to the pan and gently crush the potatoes with a fork or masher. Add the chives and season to taste with salt. Serve sprinkled with paprika, if desired.

Serves 3–4

variations

spiced oven wedges

see base recipe page 211

spiced sweet potato wedges
Follow the basic recipe, using sweet potatoes instead of baking potatoes.

lemon & thyme oven wedges
Replace the cumin with the juice of 1 lemon and 1 teaspoon dried thyme.

crispy oven wedges
Omit the paprika and cumin. Using salt flakes or roughly ground sea salt is a nice touch. Serve with mayonnaise or sour cream, if desired.

parmesan-loaded oven wedges
Omit the cumin and add 2 tablespoons grated Parmesan cheese to the spice mixture. Cook as directed. For a decadent touch, when cooked, toss in another 2 tablespoons grated Parmesan mixed with 1 tablespoon chopped parsley. Serve drizzled with sour cream and topped with bacon bits.

variations

greek salad

see base recipe page 212

loaded greek entrée salad
Make the greek salad as directed. Sit the salad on a bed of torn lettuce. Add 1/2 x 14-ounce can garbanzo beans, rinsed and drained, 1 small chopped green bell pepper, 2 tablespoons toasted whole almonds, and 1 teaspoon capers.

greek salad pita
Make the salad as directed. Toast a pita bread in the toaster until soft and puffed out. Cut in half and carefully separate the top and bottom layers of the pita to make a pocket. Stuff with the salad.

fishy greek salad
Make the greek salad as directed and top with the well drained sardines from a 3-ounce can.

greek salad with grape leaves & artichokes
Add 8 sliced sweet pickled peppers to the salad and top with 6 stuffed grape leaves and 2 marinated artichoke hearts. The ingredients can be from jars or bought from the deli counter.

italian–style broccoli

see base recipe page 215

pasta with lemon broccoli
Increase the oil to 2 tablespoons. Toss the broccoli through 2 portions cooked pasta (about 2 cups uncooked). Add Parmesan shavings to serve.

broccoli with sundried tomatoes & olives
Add 2 tablespoons chopped sundried tomatoes and 6 halved black pitted olives to the hot oil and cook for 1 minute to heat through before tossing in the broccoli. This is also good over pasta.

soy & honey broccoli
Add 1 teaspoon ginger purée with the garlic. Replace the lemon with 1 tablespoon soy sauce and 1 teaspoon runny honey.

italian–style string beans
Replace the broccoli with 8 ounces string beans. Microwave or steam as for the broccoli. Proceed as directed, adding 1 medium chopped tomato (preferably skinned and seeded).

variations

potato salad

see base recipe page 216

warm german potato salad
Cook 4 slices of smoked bacon in a large skillet over a medium-high heat until crisp and brown. Remove from the pan, crumble, and set aside. Stir 1 tablespoon all-purpose flour into the bacon fat in the skillet, then add 1 tablespoon sugar, 1/3 cup water, and 1/4 cup vinegar to the skillet and cook until the dressing is thick. Add the bacon, potatoes, onion, and parsley, stir until warm, then serve immediately. Omit the remaining ingredients.

potato, olive & tomato salad
Prepare the basic potato salad, adding 12 pitted olives and 2 medium tomatoes, cut into chunks.

lite lemony potato salad
Replace the sour cream and mayonnaise with 2 tablespoons each of olive oil and lemon juice and the grated zest of 1/2 lemon.

curried mayonnaise potato salad
Replace the sour cream with low-fat natural yogurt. Mix 1 to 2 teaspoons medium curry powder, 1/2 tablespoon mango chutney or cranberry sauce, and 1 teaspoon red chili flakes into the mayonnaise. Use to dress the potato salad. Omit the dill pickles.

variations

string beans & bacon vinaigrette

see base recipe page 218

string beans & tomato vinaigrette
Omit the bacon. Heat the olive oil in a small pan and cook the scallion for 1 minute. Add 1 chopped (preferably skinned) tomato, the vinegar and the mustard. Proceed as in the basic recipe.

string beans with lemon & almonds
Omit the bacon and vinegar. Heat the olive oil in a small pan and cook the scallion for 1 minute. Add the juice of 1 lemon and the mustard, and heat through. Proceed as in the basic recipe. Serve scattered with 2 tablespoons toasted slivered almonds.

pasta with creamy string beans & bacon
Replace the vinegar with 2 tablespoons sour cream or Greek yogurt, 1 tablespoon milk, and 2 tablespoons pasta cooking water. Toss into 2 portions cooked pasta (about 2 cups uncooked) and serve garnished with Parmesan cheese.

cabbage & bacon vinaigrette
Cook the bacon as directed and remove it from pan. Add 1/2 small sliced onion to the bacon fat plus the olive oil and sauté for 5 minutes until soft. Add 1/2 small white cabbage, shredded, 2 tablespoons water and a pinch each of sugar, salt, and pepper. Cook for about 15 minutes until the cabbage wilts. Stir in the bacon, vinegar, and mustard and heat through.

variations

seedy couscous

see base recipe page 219

couscous with tomatoes
Cook the couscous in the bouillon as directed. Omit the mixed seeds. While the couscous is resting add 2 medium chopped tomatoes (preferably seeded and skinned). If serving as a salad, add the tomatoes with the other ingredients after the couscous has cooled.

spicy couscous & garbanzo beans
Add 1/3 x 14-ounce can garbanzo beans, rinsed and drained, to the uncooked couscous. Stir 1/2 teaspoon harissa into the water with the bouillon and proceed as directed. If you haven't got harissa, use chili sauce instead.

couscous & feta fritters
Add 1/2 cup crumbled feta cheese, 1/2 beaten egg, and 1 1/2 tablespoons natural yogurt to the cooked and cooled couscous. Divide the mixture into four equal portions and shape into burgers. Heat 1 tablespoon olive oil in a skillet, then cook over a medium heat for 3 minutes on each side, or until golden.

tabbouleh
Replace the couscous with bulgur wheat and allow to stand for 1 hour. Add all the other ingredients except the seeds. Also add 1 large chopped tomato (preferably deseeded and skinned) and 4 inches (10 cm.) chopped cucumber. This dish is good served with pan-seared halloumi (page 150).

black beans & rice

see base recipe page 221

mexican beans & rice
When adding the cumin power also add 1 chopped jalapeño pepper and 1 tablespoon tomato purée.

coconut rice & beans
Replace 1/3 cup of the vegetable bouillon with reduced-fat coconut milk and add 1/2–1 teaspoon red chili flakes.

quick jambalaya
Cook 6 ounces sliced Spanish, Polish, or other spiced or smoked sausage and 1/2 green bell pepper, chopped, in the oil with the onion. Replace the cumin with 1 teaspoon Cajun spices, if available. Stir 8 large cooked shrimp into the rice instead of the beans.

rice & lentils
Replace the beans with 1/2 x 14-ounce can green lentils, rinsed and drained, or 1 cup freshly cooked green lentils. This makes a good cold salad base as well as a hot side dish.

variations

dhal with spinach

see base recipe page 222

dhal with garbanzo beans
Stir 1/2 x 14-ounce can garbanzo beans, rinsed and drained, into the almost-cooked dhal and heat through, then proceed as directed.

tomato dhal
Add 1 teaspoon tomato purée with the coconut milk and water, then add 2 medium chopped tomatoes with the spinach to heat through. Proceed as directed.

spicy lemon dhal
Add 1 chopped red chile (deseeded for a milder flavor) to the onions about 2 minutes before they are cooked. Once cooked, stir in the grated zest and juice of 1/2 lemon and proceed as directed.

dhal with egg
For an inexpensive supper make the dhal and top with 1 fried egg or 1 hard-boiled egg, peeled and cut into quarters (page 47).

herby crushed potatoes

see base recipe page 224

crushed potatoes with grainy mustard
Replace the chives with 1 to 2 tablespoons grainy mustard, to taste.

garlic crushed potatoes
Add 2 whole garlic cloves when cooking the potatoes. When drained, remove the skin and mash to a paste with a fork. Return to the pan when crushing the potatoes. Garnish with chives or chopped fresh parsley.

mashed potatoes
Replace the salad potatoes with floury potatoes such as Russet, cut into large pieces. Cook in the boiling water for about 20 minutes until very tender, but not disintegrating. Mash until smooth with a potato masher (do not be tempted to use a blender or you will end up with a glue-like texture). Add the butter and salt plus 3 to 4 tablespoons milk or light cream to get a rich, creamy texture. Stir through the chives and garnish with paprika.

chunky colcannon
While the potatoes are cooking, cook 3 slices of bacon until crispy. Remove from the pan and chop into pieces. Shred 1/4 small green cabbage. Add the butter to the bacon fat and sauté the cabbage until just tender. Crush the potatoes as directed and stir in the bacon and cabbage and 1/3 cup warmed light cream. Season with salt and pepper. Omit the paprika and chives.

something sweet

Few people can resist dessert and the recipes here are shamelessly fun and enjoyable. Still, it is best to avoid eating ice cream, cheesecake, and chocolate fondue on a daily basis. That isn't to say that healthy eating can't be pleasurable eating — the charbroiled pineapple, the spiced oranges and dates, and the summer berry crisp are sensible choices while still being delectable.

white chocolate & strawberry cheesecake in a glass

see variations page 251

This cheat's cheesecake requires no baking and can be served either as soon as it's made or kept covered in the refrigerator for a few hours (or overnight).

4 graham crackers
8 strawberries, chopped
1/3 cup cream cheese
2 tbsp. confectioners' sugar
1/4 tsp. vanilla extract

1/4 tsp. lemon juice
1/3 cup heavy cream or Greek yogurt
1 square of white chocolate, grated

Put the crackers in a plastic bag and crush them until you have chunky crumbs. Divide them equally between two glasses and press down lightly.

Reserve 1 strawberry for decoration and roughly chop the remainder. Divide the chopped strawberries between the two glasses.

Beat together the cream cheese, sugar, vanilla, lemon juice, and cream until thick. Top each glass with the mixture followed by the grated chocolate. Cut the remaining strawberry in half and use to garnish each cheesecake.

Serves 2

pears with ice cream &
hot chocolate sauce

see variations page 252

This is a quick version of the classic dessert Pears Belle Helene. The chocolate sauce is deliciously rich, thanks to the evaporated milk, and because the pears are out of a can, this is a handy recipe to have up your sleeve when you need an impromptu dessert.

4 canned pear halves
2–4 scoops of vanilla ice cream

chocolate sauce
1/4 cup bittersweet chocolate chips
1 tbsp. butter
1/2 x 14-oz. can evaporated milk
1 tbsp. superfine sugar
1/2 tsp. vanilla extract
1 tbsp. water

In a saucepan, combine all the sauce ingredients. Slowly bring to a simmer and cook, stirring, until the chocolate has melted and the ingredients are well combined.

Arrange the pears, 1 tablespoon of the pear juice and the ice cream in two dishes and pour over the hot chocolate sauce.

Serves 2

nutty chocolate mousse

see variations page 253

Serve this very rich dessert in small teacups or espresso cups. If you like your mousse light and airy, you could, after adding the cream, fold in an egg white that has been beaten until lightly stiffened; remember the usual health caveats for eating raw egg (page 88).

1/2 cup good quality chopped
   bittersweet chocolate
1 cup heavy cream
2 tbsp. water

1 cup mini marshmallows, plus
   a few more to garnish
2 tbsp. smooth peanut, almond, or
   other nut butter

Put the chocolate, 1/2 cup of the cream, the water, marshmallows, and peanut butter in a dry heatproof bowl set over a pan of simmering water. Take care not to allow the base of the bowl to make contact with the water beneath it in the pan. Stir the mixture until smooth and melted, then remove the bowl from the heat and let cool to room temperature. (You can accelerate the cooling process by sitting the bowl in cold water.)

Beat the remaining cream with a wire whisk until soft peaks form. Carefully fold the cream into the cooled chocolate mixture using a spatula or large metal spoon. Pour into bowls and chill for at least 2 hours before serving decorated with a few marshmallows.

Serves 3

icebox minis

see variations page 254

This is an indulgent no-cook recipe that should be rested overnight in the refrigerator — you better do a good job of hiding it, though! The finished result is always a delight and is a sure-fire winner every time. Choose cookies with a diameter of about 2 inches (5 cm.) to give a good-sized portion. Other good cookie choices include graham crackers, double chocolate chip cookies and shortbread cookies.

1 cup heavy cream
1 tbsp. confectioners' sugar
1/2 tsp. vanilla extract

1 packet of chocolate chip cookies
chocolate chips, M&Ms or other candies,
   to decorate

Beat the cream and sugar together with a wire whisk until soft peaks form, then stir in the vanilla. Do not over beat — the cream should still be floppy and light. Put one cookie on a large plate. Drop a rounded teaspoon of whipped cream onto the center of the cookie and flatten, leaving a rim of about 1/8 inch (3 mm.) around the outside edge of the cookie. Gently press another cookie on top of the whipped cream until the cream is flush with the edges. Continue until you have stacked six cookies to make one mini cake. Finish off with a layer of whipped cream. Repeat until the cream and cookies are used up — you should make five mini cakes.

Chill in the refrigerator for at least 6 hours, but preferably overnight, to allow the liquid from the cream to seep into the cookies. Just before serving, decorate with chocolate chips, M&Ms, or candies of your choice.

Makes about 5

almost-instant chocolate chip ice cream

see variations page 255

This ice cream is almost a science lesson in itself. It is handmade in every sense, given that the best way to chill it is to pass it from person to person to keep it churning! Tips for success: Have thick plastic freezer bags that will not tear and seal the zip-lock bags thoroughly (one leak and your efforts are in vain). Better still, secure the seal with packaging tape as well. And wear warm gloves!

1 cup whole milk
1 tbsp. superfine or confectioners' sugar
1/2 tsp. vanilla extract
1 oz. semisweet chocolate, cut into chips

6 tbsp. salt
about 1 lb. ice
ice cream sprinkles or chopped nuts (optional)

Double up two medium-sized zip-lock bags and put them in a bowl. Pour in the milk, sugar, vanilla, and chocolate chips. Seal tightly.

Take a large zip-lock bag. Add the salt and half fill with ice. Put the doubled-up medium bag into the larger bag, then seal this bag, too. Wearing gloves, pass the parcel around from person to person to freeze the ice cream — this will take up to 15 minutes. If working on your own, put the salt, ice, and bags with the milk mixture in a plastic container and keep them moving around. Serve the frozen ice cream decorated with ice cream sprinkles or chopped nuts, if desired.

Serves 2

charbroiled pineapple

see variations page 256

This is an easy cupboard dessert that is utterly delicious with a scoop of ice cream or a little Greek yogurt. It works well for breakfast, too—without the ice cream!

4 pineapple slices
2 tsp. butter, softened
2 tbsp. brown sugar

1/4 tsp. ground cinnamon or 4 pinches
   of ground ginger
Greek yogurt or ice cream, to serve

Put the pineapple slices on a broiler pan. Spread each slice with about 1/2 teaspoon butter, then sprinkle over the brown sugar and cinnamon or ginger.

Position the pineapple slices about 4 inches (10 cm.) away from the heat and broil, on one side only, for about 5 minutes until bubbling and the sugar is just beginning to take on a dark brown caramelized color. Remove from the heat, and serve warm with yogurt or ice cream.

Serves 2

spiced orange & date salad

see variations page 257

A refreshing fruit salad that brings the flavors of Morocco to your table. The oranges are served in a simple syrup that can be adapted and used for other fruits, making this a versatile recipe, too. Traditionally, a little orange flower water would be added to the syrup, but this is not essential. However, if you happen to have some, it adds a touch of authenticity.

syrup
1/4 cup sugar
1 tbsp. lemon juice
3 tbsp. water
1/4 tsp. ground cinnamon

salad
2 tbsp. slivered almonds
2-3 medium oranges, peeled and sliced
1/2 cup chopped pitted dates

Combine the syrup ingredients in a medium-sized saucepan. Bring to a boil, stirring, until the sugar has dissolved. Let cool.

Meanwhile, heat a medium-sized skillet and toast the almonds, stirring frequently, until lightly golden. Set aside to cool.

Put the orange slices in a bowl and pour over the cooled syrup. Add the dates, then leave to stand for about 30 minutes to infuse. Sprinkle over the toasted almonds to serve.

Serves 2

summer berry crisp

see variations page 258

This is such a rustic dessert and surprisingly easy to cook well. It's made with frozen fruit, which is more convenient and easier to store. However, use fresh berries if you have some that need using up.

fruit base
12-oz. package of frozen mixed berries,
    unthawed
2 tbsp. light brown sugar
1 tbsp. all-purpose flour
1 tsp. lemon juice

crisp topping
6 tbsp. light brown sugar
6 tbsp. uncooked rolled oats
1/4 cup all-purpose flour
pinch of fine salt
1/2 tsp. ground cinnamon
3 tbsp. chilled butter, cut into small pieces

Preheat the oven to 375°F (190°C). Butter a small ovenproof dish. To make the fruit base, combine the ingredients in a bowl and toss to mix. Pour the berry mixture into the prepared ovenproof dish.

For the crisp topping, combine the brown sugar, oats, flour, salt, and cinnamon in a bowl until evenly combined. With your fingertips, blend in the butter pieces until the mixture forms small clumps and the butter is well incorporated.

Sprinkle the topping evenly over the berries and bake for 30 minutes, or until the topping is crispy. Cool on a rack for at least 30 minutes before serving warm, or leave to cool to room temperature before serving.

Serves 3–4

greek yogurt with warm blueberry sauce

see variations page 259

This is another versatile recipe that can be adapted to suit your mood and the contents of your refrigerator. If serving for friends, put it into tall glasses and serve with shortbread or another butter-rich biscuit for an elegant touch.

3 1/2 oz. blueberries
1/4 cup water
2 tbsp. sugar

1 tbsp. lemon juice
1/2 tbsp. butter
1 cup fat-free Greek yogurt

Combine the blueberries, water, sugar, and lemon juice in a small pan and slowly bring to a boil. Simmer over a low heat for about 6 minutes, or until the sauce thickens. Stir in the butter, then take the pan off the heat and leave to stand for a few minutes until the mixture has cooled slightly.

Divide the yogurt between two bowls and pour over the warm sauce. Swirl with a knife to create a marbled effect.

Alternatively, make the sauce ahead of time and let cool completely, then serve it as a cold dessert.

Serves 2

apple strudel

see variations page 260

Using frozen puff pastry makes this dessert a whiz to make and it looks very impressive, too. It is one of those recipes that, once tried, will be revisited many times over the years. Serve with lightly whipped cream or with vanilla ice cream.

1 sheet of puff pastry, thawed if frozen	1/4 cup raisins
2 large Granny Smith or braeburn apples,	1 tsp. ground cinnamon
peeled cored and thinly sliced	1 tbsp. milk
juice of 1/2 lemon	2 tbsp. slivered almonds or chopped mixed nuts
1/4 cup light brown sugar	1 tbsp. confectioners' sugar

Preheat the oven to 400°F (200°C). Carefully unroll the pastry and place it on a sheet of parchment paper or an unbuttered baking sheet.

Put the sliced apple into a bowl and add the lemon juice, sugar, raisins, and cinnamon; toss to mix. Pile the apple mixture into the center of the pastry sheet. Dampen the edges of the pastry with water. Gently bring the two long edges together and seal tightly. Fold in the two short ends and press to seal. Check all the seals to ensure there are no holes. Make a few slits in the top of the pastry to allow the steam to escape.

Brush the top with milk and sprinkle over the nuts. Bake for 15 to 20 minutes, or until golden brown. Dust with sifted confectioners' sugar and serve either warm or at room temperature.

Makes 4–6 slices

microwave vanilla fudge

see variations page 261

It is good to have a simple recipe for fudge for those times when nothing but sugar will do. Fudge also makes an inexpensive gift and everybody appreciates something that has been thoughtfully and lovingly made. Wrap in clear plastic and decorate with a ribbon for the best effect.

1/2 cup (1 stick) butter, cut into pieces
1 cup superfine sugar

14-oz. can condensed milk
1 tsp. vanilla extract

Line an 8-inch- (20-cm.-) square baking pan or foil container with parchment paper.

Put the butter in the largest microwave-safe glass bowl that you have (plastic might melt). Cook the butter on HIGH in 30 second-intervals until melted. Stir in the sugar and pour in the condensed milk. Cook on HIGH for about 10 minutes, stopping every minute to stir. The cooked fudge will be golden brown. If you have a candy thermometer it should read 235-240°F (113–116°C). To check if it is ready by sight, a small amount of fudge dropped into chilled water forms a soft ball that flattens after a few seconds in your hand.

Let cool for 5 minutes, stir in the vanilla, then beat with a wooden spoon until the fudge starts to set and loses its shine. Pour the mixture into the prepared pan and leave to set before cutting it into squares.

Makes about 36 pieces

white chocolate & strawberry cheesecake in a glass

see base recipe page 235

chocolate & orange cheesecake in a glass
Replace the graham crackers with chocolate cookies. Use only a few drops of vanilla extract and replace the lemon juice with 1 teaspoon orange juice and 1 teaspoon orange zest. Replace the strawberries with the chopped flesh of 1/2 orange. Replace the white chocolate with orange-flavored chocolate.

strawberry & granola cheesecake in a glass
Replace the graham crackers with 2 tablespoons granola per glass. Omit the white chocolate and sprinkle more granola over the top of the glass before decorating the cream-cheese mixture with the halved strawberry.

raspberry & ginger cheesecake in a glass
Replace the graham crackers with ginger cookies and the strawberries with raspberries. Also, replace the white chocolate with ginger-flavored chocolate.

dairy-free strawberry & lemon cheesecake in a glass
Use vegan or dairy-free biscuits and make the cheesecake with soy-based vegan cream cheese and vegan chocolate.

variations

pears with ice cream & hot chocolate sauce

see base recipe page 236

pineapple with hot chocolate sauce

Replace the pears with 4 slices of fresh or canned pineapple. Serve with the hot chocolate sauce. Omit the ice cream.

pound cake fondue

Make the chocolate sauce and pour it into a bowl. Cut cubes of pound cake and arrange on a plate with two forks. Dip the cake into the hot sauce and eat immediately. This is delicious with chocolate cake too!

banana split with hot chocolate sauce

Make the chocolate sauce. Replace the pears with a small banana. Pour the chocolate sauce over the banana and ice cream and serve scattered with a few toasted slivered almonds.

chocolate nut sundae

Make the chocolate sauce adding 1/4 cup smooth peanut butter. In a sundae or tall glass, put one scoop of toffee ice cream, followed by one scoop of chocolate ice cream. Pour over the hot chocolate sauce and sprinkle over some chopped peanuts or pecans.

nutty chocolate mousse

see base recipe page 239

chocolate mousse
Omit the peanut butter. Add 1/4 teaspoon vanilla extract to the cooled chocolate mixture.

easy layered chocolate mousse
Replace the cream with evaporated milk and use 1 1/2 cups mini marshmallows. Omit the peanut butter. When beating the evaporated milk it will become frothy and stiff. Fold it into the cooled chocolate mixture without over-mixing — that way, the mousse separates into a creamy bottom layer and airy top layer.

mocha mousse
Replace the water with 2 tablespoons strong coffee, preferably espresso.

minty mousse
Omit the peanut butter. Add a few drops of peppermint extract for a stronger flavor or crushed mints for texture.

chocolate mousse tart
Buy a pastry tart shell and fill with the nutty chocolate mousse. Garnish with white and semisweet chocolate shavings.

icebox minis

see base recipe page 240

mocha icebox minis
Replace the vanilla with 1 tablespoon strong coffee, preferably espresso, and 1 ounce melted semisweet chocolate.

chili–chocolate icebox minis
Replace the vanilla with 1 ounce melted semisweet chocolate, 1 to 2 teaspoons chili powder and 1/4 to 1/2 teaspoon cayenne pepper. Add the chili powder a little at a time until the mixture is spicy enough for you.

strawberry–chocolate icebox minis
Add 10 finely chopped strawberries to the whipped cream. Decorate with strawberry slices instead of chocolate chips or sweets.

mango–ginger icebox minis
Replace the chocolate chip cookies with ginger cookies. Add 3 tablespoons finely chopped mango (fresh or canned) to the whipped cream. Decorate with mango slices.

almost-instant chocolate chip ice cream

see base recipe page 241

handmade vanilla ice cream
Omit the chocolate chips.

handmade chocolate ice cream
Add 2 tablespoons chocolate sauce or Nutella to the milk in the bag.

handmade blueberry ice cream
Add 1/3 cup frozen blueberries to the milk in the bag.

handmade honeycomb ice cream
Replace the chocolate with 2 ounces chocolate-coated honeycomb candy, broken into pieces, and the sugar with honey. Serve with more chocolate-coated honeycomb.

handmade lemon ice cream
Reduce the vanilla to a few drops. Add the grated zest and juice of 1/2 lemon to the bag with the milk. Increase the sugar to 2 tablespoons.

charbroiled pineapple

see base recipe page 242

charbroiled mango
Cut down both sides of 2 mangos without removing the peel. Proceed as directed, serving with a squeeze of lime juice.

charbroiled banana
Peel 2 bananas and rub each with about 1 teaspoon lemon juice. Omit the butter. Simply sprinkle with brown sugar and cinnamon or ginger. Broil as directed for 4 minutes, then turn the bananas over and broil for another 3 to 4 minutes until soft.

charbroiled peaches
Halve and stone 2 ripe peaches. Prepare and cook as directed.

charbroiled grapefruit
Halve 1 large pink or white grapefruit. Segment the grapefruit by cutting beside each of the membranes and around the inner pith. (It will be much easier to eat.) Prepare and cook as directed. Omit the cinnamon and ginger.

spiced orange & date salad

see base recipe page 245

quick orange & date salad
Omit the syrup. Pour 1/4 cup orange and mango juice over the fruit and sprinkle with ground cinnamon.

spiced orange, date & pomegranate salad
Add the seeds of 1/4 small pomegranate with the dates.

spiced peaches & dates
Replace the oranges with 2 large peaches, peeled, pitted and sliced. (To peel, submerge the peach in boiling water for 20 seconds, run under cold water to cool, then peel off the skin.)

minted oranges & strawberries
Add 8 sliced strawberries to the oranges and use 1 tablespoon chopped fresh mint instead of the cinnamon.

summer berry crisp

see base recipe page 246

apple crisp
Replace the berries with 3 large Granny Smith apples, peeled, cored and cut into 1/4-inch (5-mm.) slices. Also add 1/2 teaspoon ground cinnamon to the fruit. Make the topping and proceed as directed.

apple & pear crisp
Replace the berries with 2 large Granny Smith apples and 1 medium pear, all peeled, cored and cut into 1/4-inch (5 mm.) slices. Also add 1/2 teaspoon ground cinnamon to the fruit.

minted berry with nutty crisp
Add 1 teaspoon dried mint or 1 tablespoon chopped fresh mint to the berries. To the crisp add 2 tablespoons slivered almonds and 1 tablespoon sunflower seeds.

peach & blueberry crisp
Replace the berries with a 14-ounce can peach halves in natural juices, drained, and 1/3 cup fresh or frozen blueberries. Also add 1/2 teaspoon ground cinnamon to the base. Make the topping and proceed as directed.

variations

greek yogurt with warm blueberry sauce

see base recipe page 247

ice cream with warm raspberry sauce
Replace the blueberries with raspberries and serve over raspberry swirl ice cream.

waffles with warm blueberry sauce
Toast 4 Belgian waffles following the packet directions. Serve with warm blueberry sauce and 4 tablespoons Greek yogurt or lightly whipped cream.

double blueberry pancakes
Make the blueberry oat pancakes (page 17) and serve with the warm blueberry sauce.

blueberry & strawberry parfait
Make the blueberry sauce and let cool completely. Put 1 tablespoon granola in the base of a tall glass. Add a layer of blueberry sauce, then a layer of yogurt; repeat. Put a layer of sliced strawberries on top of the final layer of yogurt.

apple strudel

see base recipe page 248

apple & blackberry strudel
Use only 1 1/2 apples and replace the raisins with 1 1/4 cups blackberries.

sweet cheese strudel
Omit the apple filling. In a bowl combine 1/2 cup each of cream cheese and fromage frais or ricotta cheese, both at room temperature. Beat in 1 egg, 1/2 cup superfine sugar and 1 teaspoon vanilla extract. Stir in 1/4 cup raisins. Construct the strudel as directed.

french apple tart
Prepare the pastry as directed. Core, then slice, 4 unpeeled braeburn apples and toss in the lemon juice. Slightly overlap the apple slices in rows on top of the pastry, leaving a 2-inch (5-cm.) gap around the edges. Drizzle 2 tablespoons melted butter over the apples, sprinkle with 1/4 cup superfine sugar and dust with cinnamon. Brush the pastry edges with milk and fold the edges inward, pressing down to form a crust. Bake as directed.

applesauce
Combine the apples, lemon, sugar, and cinnamon in a medium pan. Cook over a moderate heat, stirring often, until the apples are tender but holding their shape. For smooth applesauce, cook for a little longer and beat with a wooden spoon until puréed.

microwave vanilla fudge

see base recipe page 250

sour cherry fudge
Add 1/4 cup chopped sour cherries just before pouring the fudge into the prepared pan.

coconut fudge
Add 3 tablespoons dried or shredded coconut with the vanilla.

chocolate fudge
Add 3 tablespoons cocoa powder to the sugar when cooking the fudge.

pecan fudge
Add 3/4 cup chopped pecans just before pouring the fudge into the prepared pan.

stove-top fudge
Put the ingredients into a large non-stick saucepan and melt over a low heat, stirring until the sugar dissolves. Bring to a boil, then simmer for 10 to 15 minutes, stirring continuously with a wooden spoon to prevent the fudge from sticking and burning at the base and in the corners of the pan. Take care — the mixture is very hot. Test and finish as directed.

a bit of baking

Baking can be daunting when you are new to cooking, but these recipes have been selected for their ease and reliability. If you don't have a food mixer, beating can be done by hand — not a problem with the brownies and muffins, and the birthday cake contains oil, reducing the need for vigorous beating. You still get an arm-muscle workout, but only a mini one. To really cheat, make the tiffin — it requires no baking and is ridiculously addictive.

fudgy brownies

see variations page 276

This is a classic. The trick with brownies is not to over-bake; you need to take them out of the oven as soon as they pull away from the sides of the pan, while the center is still soft. Served warm, they are delicious as a dessert with a few strawberries and some ice cream, but they are equally delicious cold with a glass of milk.

1/3 cup (2/3 stick) butter	2 eggs
1/2 cup semisweet chocolate, chopped	1/2 tsp. vanilla extract
1 cup superfine sugar	2/3 cup self-rising flour

Preheat the oven to 350°F (175°C). Grease an 8 x 8-inch (20 x 20-cm.) cake pan and line it with parchment paper.

Put the butter and chocolate in a medium-sized pan and melt over a low heat, stirring occasionally. Remove it from the heat. Using a wooden spoon, beat in the sugar, eggs, and vanilla. Stir in the flour.

Pour the batter into the prepared pan and bake for 25 to 30 minutes, or until the edges and top are set but the mixture feels soft underneath. Cool for 15 minutes, then slice into bars and remove from the pan. Finish cooling on a wire rack.

Makes 9 or 12 bars

vanilla birthday cake

see variations page 277

Having a celebration cake recipe is a must for everyone. What nicer present could you give to someone than a personalized birthday cake? You can customize the decoration to suit the personality and add a candle or two for good effect. However, don't save this recipe just for special occasions—it is lovely to eat at any time.

1 cup superfine sugar
4 eggs
2 1/2 cups self-rising flour
3/4 cup sunflower oil
2/3 cup milk
1 1/2 tsp. vanilla extract
sprinkles or other cake decorations, to decorate

frosting
3 cups confectioners' sugar, sifted
1/3 cup (2/3 stick) butter, at room temperature
1 1/2 tsp. vanilla extract
about 2 tbsp. milk

Preheat the oven to 350°F (175°C). Line two 9-inch (23-cm.) round cake pans or one 13 x 9-inch (33 x 23-cm.) pan with parchment paper. Grease the paper and the sides of the pan with a little oil or butter.

In a large mixing bowl and with a wire whisk, beat the sugar and eggs together for 4 to 5 minutes (or about 1 minute with a food mixer) until slightly thickened. Add the flour, oil, milk, and vanilla and beat until the batter is smooth and creamy. Pour the batter into the prepared baking pans. Bake for 30 to 35 minutes for the round cakes, 35 to 40 minutes for the oblong cake; the tops should be golden and a toothpick inserted into the center of the cake should come out clean. Rest for 5 minutes. Loosen the sides of the cake from the pan using a knife, then turn out onto a wire rack and peel off the paper. Allow to cool.

To make the frosting, mix the confectioners' sugar and butter together with a soft spatula or spoon. Stir in the vanilla and sufficient milk to give the mixture a spreadable consistency. Spread just under half the frosting over the top of one cake, top with the other layer and spread the remaining frosting over the top. Decorate with sprinkles or other cake decorations.

Serves 12

cranberry oat bars

see variations page 278

An oat bar is a wonderful thing to eat as a snack and it is easy to transport sealed in a little plastic wrap. What's more, these homemade oat bars are simple to make and they cost a fraction of what those fancy oat bars served in coffee shops do.

1/2 cup (1 stick) butter or dairy-free spread
1 1/4 cups light brown sugar
3 tbsp. light corn syrup, maple syrup or honey

1 heaped cup rolled oats
1/4 cup dried cranberries
3 tbsp. pumpkin seeds

Preheat the oven to 350°F (175°C). Grease an 8 x 8-inch (20 x 20-cm.) cake pan and line it with parchment paper.

Put the butter, sugar, and syrup in a medium-sized pan and melt over a low heat, stirring occasionally. Remove from the heat and stir in the oats, cranberries, and pumpkin seeds.

Pour the mixture into the prepared pan and bake for 15 to 20 minutes, or until just beginning to turn golden — do not over-cook. Cool for 5 minutes, then slice into bars and remove from the pan. Finish cooling on a wire rack.

To cook in the microwave: put the butter, sugar, and syrup in a microwave-safe bowl and cook on HIGH for 1 to 2 minutes or until the butter has melted. Stir in the oats, cranberries, and seeds and mix thoroughly. Press into a small greased or parchment paper-lined microwave-safe baking dish. Cook on HIGH for about 5 minutes or until the center is bubbling.

Makes 9 or 12 bars

chocolate chip cookies

see variations page 279

Some foods deserve their fine reputation, and this is one of them. If you are going to master any cookie, let it be this one. The crunchy nuts and soft chocolate make these irresistible, especially with a glass of ice-cold milk. The dough can be stored, covered, in the refrigerator for up to five days, so you can have fresh cookies whenever you want.

1/4 cup (1/2 stick) butter, at room temperature
1/4 cup superfine sugar
1/3 cup brown sugar
1 egg, lightly beaten
1/2 tsp. vanilla extract

1 1/4 cups self-rising flour, sifted
1 cup chocolate chips
1/2 cup chopped pecans

Preheat the oven to 375°F (190°C). Grease a cookie sheet with a little oil or butter or line with baking parchment.

In a large mixing bowl and using a wooden spoon, beat together the butter and superfine and brown sugars until soft and fluffy (this will take about 5 minutes by hand). Add the egg and beat well to combine, then stir in the vanilla extract. Now gently fold the sifted flour into the batter with a metal spoon or spatula, taking care not to lose all the lightness you have beaten into the batter. Carefully fold in the chocolate chips and nuts.

Drop the mixture by rounded teaspoon onto the prepared cookie sheet, leaving plenty of room between the rounds to allow them to spread while they cook. Bake for 8 to 10 minutes.

Unless you have several cookie sheets, you will have to cook them in batches. If you want larger cookies, use a rounded tablespoon and cook for a couple of minutes longer.

Makes about 30 x 2-in. (5-cm.) cookies

moist banana muffins

see variations page 280

The natural sweetness and moisture in bananas means that you can reduce the sugar in these muffins without noticing. They can be made healthier still by using whole wheat flour, as shown in the variations. Unfortunately, you can't get away without buying a muffin pan, but as you always use paper muffin liners for making muffins, you don't have to buy an expensive one.

1 3/4 cups all-purpose flour
1 tsp. baking soda
1/2 tsp. baking powder
1/2 tsp. salt

3 large ripe bananas, mashed
1 cup superfine sugar
1 egg
scant 1/3 cup (2/3 stick) butter, melted

Preheat the oven to 350°F (175°C). Put 12 muffin paper liners into the cups of a 12-cup muffin pan.

Sift together the flour, baking soda, baking powder, and salt and set aside.

In a large bowl, combine the banana, sugar, egg, and melted butter. Fold in the flour mixture and mix until the ingredients are combined but the batter is still slightly lumpy; do not over-mix or the muffins will be heavy. Spoon evenly into the paper liners in the muffin pan.

Bake for 25 to 30 minutes, or until the muffins are well risen and spring back when lightly tapped. Cool for 5 minutes, then turn out onto a wire rack to cool completely.

Makes 12

cinnamon palmiers

see variations page 281

Palmiers look really impressive, but are deceptively simple to make. This version is a quick and easy variation of the French classic. Serve at the end of a meal or take them to a potluck party.

1 sheet of puff pastry, thawed
3 tbsp. brown sugar

1 tsp. ground cinnamon
flour, for dusting

Preheat the oven to 425°F (220°C). Grease 1 or 2 baking sheets with oil or line them with parchment paper.

Put the pastry on a floured surface. Sprinkle 2 tablespoons of the brown sugar over the surface of the pastry, then dust with two-thirds of the cinnamon. Fold each of the short sides of the pastry into the center; press down and sprinkle over the remaining sugar and cinnamon. Again, fold each pastry side in half so that they meet in the center. Brush the pastry with cold water and fold over to make a long roll.

Cut across the roll to make roughly 1/4 inch (5 mm.) slices (this is best done with a serrated knife), then transfer the slices to the baking sheet, leaving 1-inch (2.5-cm.) between each one to allow room for spreading. Bake for about 10 minutes, or until golden. Remove from the baking sheet with a metal spatula and cool on a wire rack. These are best eaten on the day they are made, when they are really crisp, but will store for a few days in an airtight container.

Makes 18–20

tiffin

see variations page 282

A recipe for the most nervous of bakers—all you have to do is melt the chocolate and sugar and crush a few cookies and you have a cake you can be proud of! Beware—these cookies are extremely high in calories, so don't make them too often and do share them!

1/2 cup (1 stick) butter or hard margarine
    (low-fat soft margarine will not set)
2 tbsp. light brown sugar
1/4 cup cocoa powder
1/4 cup light corn syrup

2 cups graham cracker crumbs
    (about 16 crackers)
1/3 cup raisins
1/4 cup dried cranberries

In a saucepan over a medium-low heat, melt together the butter, sugar, cocoa powder, and syrup until the sugar crystals have disappeared. Stir in the crushed crackers, the raisins, and the cranberries.

Line an 8-inch (20-cm.) square cake pan with plastic wrap. Press the mixture into the pan and flatten the surface with the back of a spoon. Using the tip of a knife, mark the surface into squares, then let set in a cool place. Slice when cooled, using your score marks to guide you.

Note: You can add a topping made from 2/3 cup melted semisweet chocolate, spread over the bars and set before slicing, if desired.

Makes 9 or 12 slices

coffee & walnut mug cake

see variations page 283

Mug cakes are becoming really popular — the idea of creating a one-person cake in a few moments is almost irresistible.

2 tbsp. melted butter
1/4 tsp. instant coffee
1/2 tsp. warm water
2 tbsp. superfine sugar or brown sugar
2 tbsp. beaten egg (about 1/2 egg)
2 tbsp. all-purpose flour
1/4 tsp. baking powder
3 walnut halves, finely chopped

frosting
1/4 tsp. instant coffee
1/4 tsp. warm water
1 1/2 tsp. butter, at room temperature
1 1/2 tbsp. confectioners' sugar, sifted
piece of walnut, for decoration

Select a mug with a capacity of 1 to 1 1/4 cups. Put the butter in the mug and melt it in the microwave on HIGH for 20 to 30 seconds. Carefully swirl the butter around the inside of the mug to grease the sides.

To make the cake batter, dissolve the instant coffee in the water, then add the coffee to the melted butter in the mug. Add all of the remaining ingredients and beat the mixture to a smooth batter using a fork. Put the mug back into the microwave and cook on HIGH for 1 minute and 20 seconds. Leave the mug to stand in the microwave without opening the door for 1 minute. Let cool. If desired, you can remove the cake from the mug after 5 minutes and continue to cool on a wire rack.

To make the frosting, dissolve the instant coffee in the water, then beat all the ingredients together with a fork until the mixture is smooth. Use to decorate the cooled cake and top with a piece of walnut.

Note: Microwave times may vary slightly. Add an additional 20 to 30 seconds for a machine under 1000 watts.

Makes 1

variations

fudgy brownies

see base recipe page 263

nutty brownies

After adding the flour, stir in 1/2 cup chopped nuts. Try pecans, walnuts, macadamia, or mixed nuts — they all work well.

peanut butter brownies

Stir in 2 tablespoons peanut butter with the vanilla and 1/4 cup chopped unsalted peanuts after the flour.

marshmallow brownies

Stir in 1 cup mini marshmallows after the flour.

double chocolate brownies

Stir in 1/2 cup white chocolate chips after the flour. Or use a selection of white, milk, and semisweet chocolate chips.

vanilla birthday cake

see base recipe page 264

vanilla cake with chocolate frosting
Replace the vanilla frosting with chocolate frosting. Mix 1/2 cup melted and cooled semisweet chocolate into the butter, then stir into the sugar. Reduce the vanilla to 1 teaspoon.

vanilla cake with cream & strawberries
Beat 3 1/2 cups cream until thickened. Sweeten to taste with 2 to 4 tablespoons sifted confectioners' sugar and stir in a few drops of vanilla extract. Spread half the cream over the cake. Add a layer of sliced strawberries. Top with the other cake and repeat. You'll need about 2 cups strawberries for the filling.

chocolate cake with vanilla frosting
When making the cake, replace 1/4 cup of the flour with 1/4 cup sifted cocoa powder. This is good with the chocolate frosting too.

orange cake
Replace the vanilla with the grated zest of 1 orange. Squeeze the juice of the orange into a measuring cup and add enough milk to yield 2/3 cup of liquid. For the frosting, use 1 teaspoon grated orange zest and replace the milk with orange juice. Omit the vanilla.

vanilla cupcakes
Put paper cupcake liners in a muffin pan. Half-fill each liner with the batter; bake for 20 minutes. Decorate with the frosting when cooled. Makes about 18.

variations

cranberry oat bars

see base recipe page 267

chocolate-coated oat bars
Melt 1 cup chopped semisweet chocolate in the microwave on HIGH in short 20-second intervals, stirring between each interval, until melted and smooth. Pour the melted chocolate over the cooled oat bars. When the chocolate is partially set, score the top of the oat bars into squares to make slicing easier.

raisin & pecan oat bars
Replace the cranberries with raisins and the pumpkin seeds with chopped pecans.

sour cherry & coconut oat bars
Replace cranberries and pumpkin seeds with a scant 1/4 cup dried shredded coconut and 1/4 cup chopped sour cherries.

ginger oat bars
Add 2 teaspoons ground ginger to the mixture. Replace the cranberries with chopped crystallized ginger.

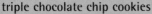
variations

chocolate chip cookies

see base recipe page 268

triple chocolate chip cookies
Add 2 tablespoons cocoa powder into the flour mixture. Use 1/2 cup each of semisweet chocolate chips and white chocolate chips.

raisin & orange cookies
Replace the chocolate chips with 3/4 cup raisins. Reduce the vanilla to 1/4 teaspoon and add the grated zest of 1 orange into the mixture with the vanilla.

granola cookies
Replace the chocolate chips and nuts with 1 cup granola.

chocolate chip cookie bars
Preheat the oven to 350°F (175°C). Line an 8 x 8-inch (20 x 20-cm.) cake pan with parchment paper and grease the sides of the pan. Make the dough as directed and spread it into the prepared pan. Bake for 20 to 30 minutes, or until golden brown and a wooden toothpick inserted into the center comes out clean. Do not over-bake. Cool on wire rack. Cut into 9 or 12 bars. Remove from the pan.

variations

moist banana muffins

see base recipe page 270

chunky whole food banana muffins
Use only 1/2 cup all-purpose flour and add 1/2 cup whole wheat flour. Mash 2 bananas and chop the third into small pieces.

cinnamon banana nut muffins
Sift 1 teaspoon ground cinnamon in with the flour. Stir 3/4 cup chopped pecans, walnuts or mixed nuts into the mixture with the other ingredients.

banana chocolate chip muffins
Stir 1/2 cup semisweet chocolate chips into the mixture with the other ingredients.

banana crunch muffins
Mix 3 tablespoons granola into the mixture with the other ingredients.

cinnamon palmiers

see base recipe page 271

nutella palmiers
Omit the sugar and cinnamon and spread the pastry with a thin layer of Nutella or other chocolate paste (about 6 tablespoons).

raspberry & orange palmiers
Omit the sugar and cinnamon and spread the pastry with a thin layer of raspberry conserve (about 6 tablespoons) and the grated zest of 1/2 orange.

pesto palmiers
Omit the sugar and cinnamon and spread the pastry with a thin layer of pesto (about 6 tablespoons) and 2 tablespoons grated Parmesan cheese.

parmesan oliver twists
Omit the sugar and cinnamon and spread the pastry with a thin layer tapenade (olive paste), (about 6 tablespoons) and 2 tablespoons grated Parmesan cheese.

variations

tiffin

see base recipe page 273

rocky road slice
Follow the basic recipe but omit the raisins and cranberries. Use instead 3 tablespoons each of mini marshmallows, white chocolate chips, and unsalted peanut halves.

two-chocolate macadamia slice
Follow the basic recipe but omit the raisins and the cranberries. Use instead 1/2 cup each of white chocolate chips and chopped macadamia nuts.

chocolate & cherry slice
Follow the basic recipe but omit the raisins and cranberries. Use instead 1/4 cup dried sour cherries and 3/4 cup slivered almonds.

chocolate, coconut & cranberry slice
Follow the basic recipe but omit the raisins. Use instead 1/2 cup dried shredded coconut and 1/2 cup dried cranberries.

variations

coffee & walnut mug cake

see base recipe page 274

coffee & chocolate chip mug cake
Replace the walnuts with 2 tablespoons semisweet chocolate chips.

mocha mug cake
Replace the walnuts with 1/2 teaspoon cocoa powder. Decorate the cake with little chocolates.

lemon drizzle mug cake
Omit the coffee and water. Add 1/4 teaspoon grated lemon zest and 1 teaspoon lemon juice to the cake batter. Replace the frosting with a drizzle made from 1 teaspoon sugar mixed with 1 teaspoon lemon juice. Drizzle this over the cake while still warm.

chocolate & walnut mug cake
Omit the coffee and water from both the cake and the frosting. Add 1 teaspoon cocoa powder with the other cake ingredients. Add 1/2 tablespoon melted chocolate chips to the frosting.

index